SAP® ERP User Guide— Tips to Increase Productivity

Sydnie McConnell

Thank you for purchasing this book from Espresso Tutorials!

Like a cup of espresso coffee, Espresso Tutorials SAP books are concise and effective. We know that your time is valuable and we deliver information in a succinct and straightforward manner. It only takes our readers a short amount of time to consume SAP concepts. Our books are well recognized in the industry for leveraging tutorial-style instruction and videos to show you step by step how to successfully work with SAP.

Check out our YouTube channel to watch our videos at
https://www.youtube.com/user/EspressoTutorials.

If you are interested in SAP Finance and Controlling, join us at
http://www.fico-forum.com/forum2/
to get your SAP questions answered and contribute to discussions.

Related titles from Espresso Tutorials:

- Boris Rubarth: First Steps in ABAP®
  http://5015.espresso-tutorials.com
- Anurag Barua: First Steps in SAP® Crystal Reports for Business Users
  http://5017.espresso-tutorials.com
- Claudia Jost: First Steps in the SAP® Purchasing Processes (MM)
  http://5016.espresso-tutorials.com
- Björn Weber: First Steps in the SAP® Production Processes (PP)
  http://5027.espresso-tutorials.com
- Sydnie McConnell & Martin Munzel: First Steps in SAP®
  (2nd, extended edition)
  http://5045.espresso-tutorials.com
- Ashish Sampat: First Steps in SAP® Controlling (CO)
  http://5069.espresso-tutorials.com
- Gerardo di Giuseppe: First Steps in SAP® Business Warehouse (BW)
  http://5088.espresso-tutorials.com
- Ann Cacciottolli: First Steps in SAP® Financial Accounting (FI)
  http://5095.espresso-tutorials.com

Sydnie McConnell
SAP® ERP User Guide—Tips to Increase Productivity

ISBN:	9-781-5369-9099-7
Editor:	Lisa Jackson
Cover Design:	Philip Esch, Martin Munzel
Cover Photo:	istockphoto # 42304422 © Picsfive
Interior Design:	Johann-Christian Hanke

All rights reserved.

1st Edition 2016, Gleichen

© 2016 by Espresso Tutorials GmbH

URL: *www.espresso-tutorials.com*

Feedback
We greatly appreciate any kind of feedback you have concerning this book. Please mail us at *info@espresso-tutorials.com*.

Table of Contents

Introduction

Over 15-plus years as both a business user and an IT analyst, I've gathered lots of tips and tricks for navigating through SAP systems. I've picked up information from so many sources: books, online searches, generous coworkers, trial and error, and so on. I've always thought it would be great to have a central source to keep track of all of these lessons, and this book is the result. While it's impossible to include every possible tool, this represents a good collection of helpful tips for every level of user, beginner to expert.

This book will help you navigate and work with SAP ERP systems more efficiently and effectively. Some of the tips may depend on the particular ERP or GUI version that you are using, but many of them will translate across different versions. I will focus primarily on SAP ERP, but most of these techniques will also be useful in different SAP products. Additionally, while most of the techniques here are useful across SAP modules, a few of them are specific to a particular module. By the same token, the vast majority of techniques here are geared toward business functionality, but there are a few configuration techniques as well.

For any task you need to perform, you will most likely have multiple options for how to do it. You may prefer to navigate to a transaction through a menu path, while your colleague may like to enter the transaction code directly. You may prefer to use your mouse to click buttons, while another colleague may want to use keyboard shortcuts. This book will help each of you find tips and tricks on how to do things more quickly and efficiently, and how to find some new ways to get around an SAP system. I hope you find something useful here, and I welcome your feedback and hearing about your favorite tips and tricks.

I would like to take the opportunity to thank my family, particularly Pat, Nancy and Tina, for always supporting and inspiring me, and putting up with my sometimes goofy ideas and schedule. My colleagues and coworkers have all been tremendously helpful over the years, teaching me new tips and tricks and sharing information, and I'm so thankful for the opportunity to work with all of them. Special thanks to Samantha Cunningham, John Johnston, Kari Legler, Buck Marshall, and Braden Nelson for contributing their favorite tips for me to include in this book. I'm particularly grateful to the team at Espresso Tutorials, for the opportunity to write and for being so wonderful to work with. Thanks for letting me be part of the team! Finally, thanks to my pack of wild dogs, who are always happy to keep my feet warm while I write, and even happier when it's time to take a break and play outside.

We have added a few icons to highlight important information. These include:

Tips

Tips highlight information concerning more details about the subject being described and/or additional background information.

Examples

Examples help illustrate a topic better by relating it to real world scenarios.

Attention

Attention notices draw attention to information that you should be aware of when you go through the examples from this book on your own.

Finally, a note concerning the copyright: all screenshots printed in this book are the copyright of SAP SE. All rights are reserved by SAP SE. Copyright pertains to all SAP images in this publication. For simplification, we will not mention this specifically underneath every screenshot.

1 Customizing your user interface

Before I discuss navigation and transactions, you will first need to log into the system and set (or change) your password. Then I'll show you options to customize the user interface. These options can help you easily differentiate between systems and enhance readability.

1.1 Logging in

The first time you log into an SAP system, you will use the user ID and temporary password given to you from your system administrator. You'll also have an SAP logon (see Figure 1.1) installed on your computer with a list of systems you have access to. In some cases, you may have access to a production system, a test system, a development system, or others.

Figure 1.1: SAP logon

Double click on the appropriate option. Enter your username and temporary password, then you'll be prompted to create a new password (Figure 1.2).

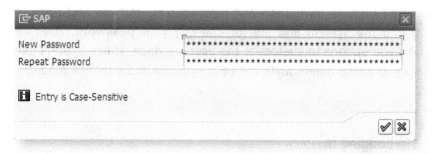

Figure 1.2: New password

Generally, your system administrator will have defined password requirements, such as the length it needs to be and special characters to include (or not). Enter your new password, twice, to validate that you've entered the correct information.

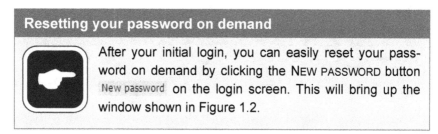

Resetting your password on demand

After your initial login, you can easily reset your password on demand by clicking the NEW PASSWORD button New password on the login screen. This will bring up the window shown in Figure 1.2.

Along with the username and password fields on the SAP logon screen, you'll also see a field for CLIENT and a field for LOGON LANGUAGE. The client will be defined by your system administrator, and it will typically be filled in with a default value. The available logon languages will depend on which language packages have been installed for your system (also defined by your system administrator). You may have the choice of logging into SAP in English or German, for example.

1.2 Visual options

Once you've logged into SAP, you can start to customize your screen by choosing themes, colors, fonts, and other helpful settings. To adjust the options discussed in this section, you will click the CUSTOMIZE LOCAL LAYOUT button 🖼, then choose OPTIONS. You can also use the keyboard shortcut [Alt] + [F12]. This will open up the SAP GUI Options window (see Figure 1.3).

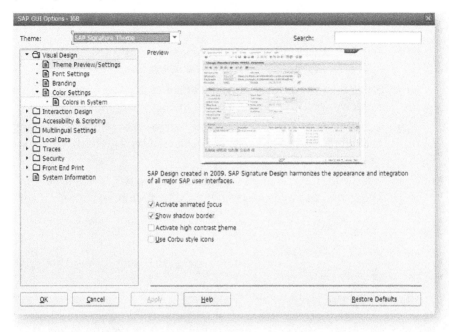

Figure 1.3: SAP GUI Options window

1.2.1 Themes

As shown in Figure 1.4, the first option under VISUAL DESIGN is the selection for THEME PREVIEW/SETTINGS. You will also see the dropdown box to choose a *theme* ❶.

Options for different themes

All of the VISUAL DESIGN options available will depend on the theme you've chosen and the options your system administrator has made available to you. I will focus primarily on the SAP SIGNATURE THEME and the options available with it, but keep in mind that you can change the theme and find other design options.

11

If you choose a different theme, you will see a preview picture ❷ and description ❸ of the theme in the right-hand frame. Depending on the theme you choose, you may also have additional choices for borders and contrast, such as:

▶ ACTIVATE ANIMATED FOCUS provides small red corners around the active field to make it easier to see where your cursor is.

▶ SHOW SHADOW BORDER provides a nice shadow around your SAP windows. You can deactivate this to improve performance.

▶ ACTIVATE HIGH CONTRAST THEME changes the display to a black background with white lettering. This can be a great option for vision-impaired users.

▶ USE CORBU STYLE gives you a set of updated system buttons. These are also available with the Corbu theme.

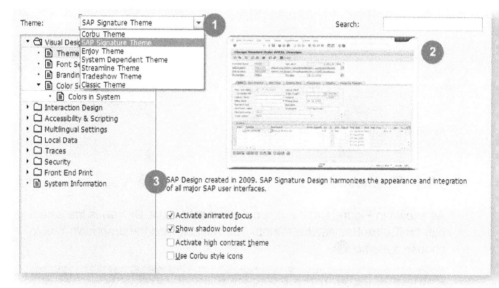

Figure 1.4: Choosing a visual theme

Finding your cursor position

When you select ACTIVATE ANIMATED FOCUS, you can press the ⌈Ctrl⌉ button to highlight and bring attention to exactly where your cursor is on the screen.

1.2.2 Font settings

The next option under VISUAL DESIGN is FONT SETTINGS. Here, you can change the font style and size in your SAP system (see Figure 1.15).

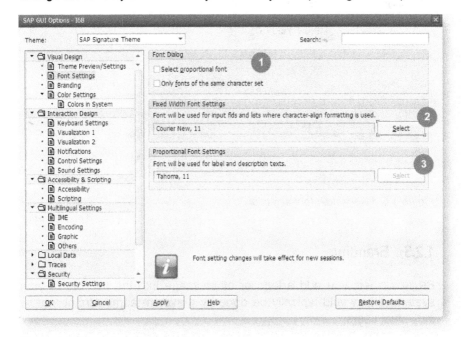

Figure 1.5: Choosing display fonts

In Figure 1.5, you see two selection boxes. ❶ One is SELECT PROPOR-TIONAL FONT and the other is ONLY FONTS OF THE SAME CHARACTER SET. Checking the box for SELECT PROPORTIONAL FONT will allow you to choose a new proportional font, i.e. a font that will use a different width for each letter (only what that letter needs), rather than fixed-width font, where each letter takes up the same amount of space. ONLY FONTS OF THE SAME CHARACTER SET will limit the fonts available. For example, if you check this box, a symbol-only font, like Webdings, would not be available.

You'll have the choice of setting a fixed-width font ❷ and a proportional font ❸. Some reports will use the fixed-width font, while many menus, labels, and fields will use the proportional font. To choose your own display font, click on the SELECT button [Select]. You'll see a window (see Figure 1.6 with choices of different font styles and sizes). Choose the option that best suits you, then click the OK button [OK].

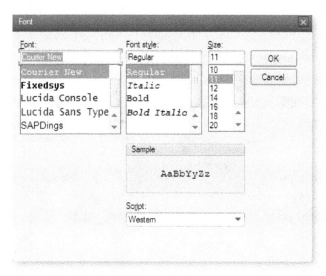

Figure 1.6: Fixed-width font selection

1.2.3 Branding

BRANDING lets you add a logo or other image into the title bar in your system. This would typically be done by a system administrator, not by individual users.

1.2.4 Color settings

With COLOR SETTINGS, you can change the display color of your SAP system (see Figure 1.7). This is another area where the options can vary greatly depending on your chosen theme and the options provided by your system administrator.

In Figure 1.7, you can see the list of available color combinations ❶ and a preview of how they look. If you don't like the color blue, you can choose a different color to make your system more visually pleasing to you. Your system administrator may have defined a backend system color. By checking the box for ACCEPT DEFAULT COLOR DEFINED BY SAP SYSTEM ❷, you will let your system default be the color defined by your administrator.

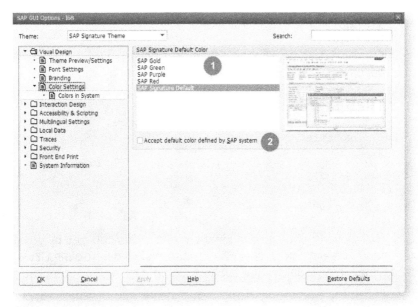

Figure 1.7: Color settings

Different colors for different systems

 Do you work in more than one system, e.g. a production system and a QA (or test) system? If so, it can be difficult to remember at first glance which system you're working in. If you're testing a new process, you want to make sure that you're working in your QA system. Use the COLORS IN SYSTEM settings to make each of your clients a different color. This provides an instant easy visual cue to you to make sure you're logged into the right system.

1.3   Other personalization options

Along with the visual options discussed in Section 1.2, you can find several other options to customize your user interface. I'll discuss a few of them here. I won't go into all of the options available, but you can test them out in your system to see how you like them.

1.3.1 Tooltip

In many applications, including SAP, you can hover your cursor over a field or option and find a label with a brief description of what it does. In SAP, this is called a TOOLTIP (see Figure 1.18).

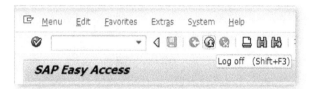

Figure 1.8: Tooltip for the log off button

In SAP GUI Options, you can change the way a tooltip behaves by going to the menu INTERACTION DESIGN • NOTIFICATIONS. Under TOOLTIP DELAY, you can change how quickly the tooltip pops up, or turn it off completely (see Figure 1.9).

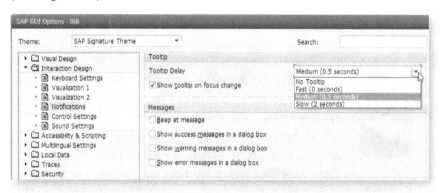

Figure 1.9: Notification options for tooltip and messages

Show tooltip on focus change

By default, you'll see a tooltip only when you hover your mouse over a button or field. If you check the box for SHOW TOOLTIP ON FOCUS CHANGE, you can use the ⬚ button to navigate through fields and buttons, and you'll see a tooltip each time you move to a new focus.

1.3.2 Messages

By default, your system will display message notifications at the bottom left of the SAP window. Depending on whether the message is an information, warning, or error message, you will see a different color box (see Figure 1.10).

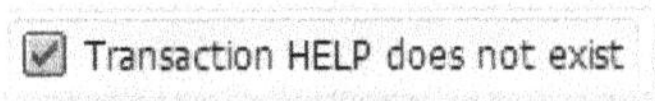

Transaction HELP does not exist

Figure 1.10: Information message about incorrect transaction code

If you want to call more attention to messages, you can use the checkboxes in the message section (shown in Figure 1.9). This can cause the message to pop up in a separate window or dialog box, requiring you or the user to acknowledge the message before proceeding, as shown in Figure 1.11. It can also provide an aural notification of any message.

Information
Transaction HELP does not exist
OK
Help

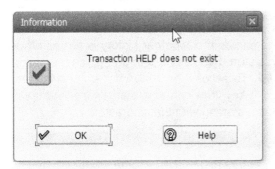

Figure 1.11: Information message dialog box

1.3.3 Sound settings

Under SOUND SETTINGS, you can check a box for ACTIVATE AUDIO FEEDBACK (Figure 1.12). This will give you a little beep or chime to confirm any activity in your SAP screen, such as opening a menu item or hitting the `Enter` key. If you want to turn off the sound without muting your entire computer, you can simple uncheck this box.

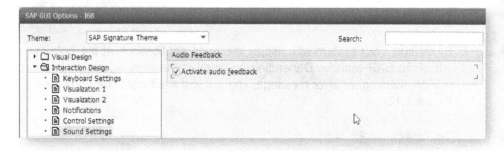

Figure 1.12: Activate audio feedback

1.3.4   History

SAP can keep all of your input history for a period of time and autofill an entry field, which can save keystrokes when entering your username, a material number, a document number, or any number of other entries. To adjust your history settings, you can navigate to LOCAL DATA • HISTORY (Figure 1.13). These settings can control whether history is turned off or on ❶, how long the history is stored ❷, along with giving you the option to clear all of your history ❸. To access the history for a specific field, you can simply hit the ⟵ key. You can also start typing and it will show you history for everything, starting with that character.

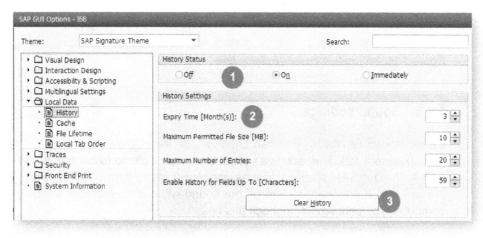

Figure 1.13: History settings

> ### Deleting a single entry from your history
>
> Sometimes you may want to delete a single entry from history for a certain field, without clearing all history. For example, you might have accidentally entered your password instead of your user ID (see Figure 1.14), and you want to make sure that doesn't show up on your screen every time you log in. To delete that single line, simply right click on the entry and hit the `Delete` key on your keyboard.

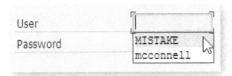

Figure 1.14: How to delete a single entry from field history

1.4   Review and quick reference

In this chapter, you looked at how to log onto an SAP system and change your password, and personalize the look and sound of your SAP system. You also learned how to manage the history settings to show past entries in different SAP fields, and how to make your production system a different color than your QA system.

Figure 1.15 has a quick reference table for the buttons and keyboard shortcuts used in this chapter.

Button	Keyboard Shortcut	Function
New password	F5	Change password
🗐	Alt + F12	Customize local layout: change colors, fonts, history settings, sound, etc.

Figure 1.15: Quick reference for buttons and keyboard shortcuts

2 Navigation

Next, you'll learn how to navigate in SAP ERP. You'll start with the screen layout and buttons, along with keyboard shortcuts, then look at the menus and transaction codes.

2.1 SAP screen

The SAP window has six basic elements: the MENU BAR, the SYSTEM FUNCTION BAR, the TITLE BAR, the APPLICATION TOOLBAR, the DYNPRO AREA (main body of the screen), and the STATUS BAR (see Figure 2.1).

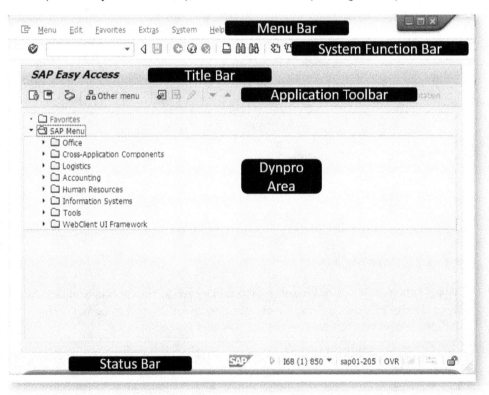

Figure 2.1 SAP screen elements

2.1.1 Menu bar

At the very top of the screen, you will find the *menu bar*. Some of the items on the menu may change depending on your transaction, but you will always see the menus for SYSTEM and HELP.

Navigating through the SAP menu is similar to many other programs. If you click on an item in the menu, you will see additional options under that item (see Figure 2.2). Some menu items also show you ❶ keyboard shortcuts, which can be used in place of navigating through the menu path. When you see ❷ a triangle pointing to the right ▶, it indicates additional menu selections. You can see the additional selections by hovering over the item in the menu.

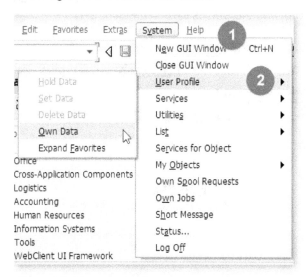

Figure 2.2: Menu navigation

The SYSTEM menu contains some general system functions and transactions. Some of these will be accessible only by your system administrator, depending on your company's policies and procedures.

Here are a couple of the most useful tools found in the SYSTEM menu:

▶ NEW GUI WINDOW: Opens a new SAP window so that you can work with multiple transactions at the same time. As a default, you can open as many as 6 sessions at once, but your system administrator may change this. You can also access this functionality with keyboard shortcut ⌈Ctrl⌉ + ⌈N⌉, or with the CREATES NEW SESSION button ▦.

▶ USER PROFILE • OWN DATA: This opens up the MAINTAIN USER PROFILE screen, also accessible through transaction SU3. Here is another spot where you can change your password by using the keyboard shortcut ⌈F6⌉ or by clicking the 🔒Password button. In the DEFAULTS tab (see Figure 2.3), you can set defaults such as ❶ printer (OUTPUTDEVICE) and ❷ print options, ❸ time zone, ❹ decimal notation, and ❺ date format. PARAMETERS will be discussed in a later chapter.

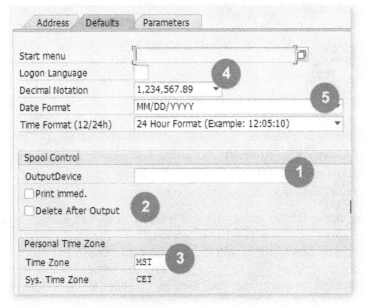

Figure 2.3: Maintain user profile—default options

The HELP menu can take you to APPLICATION HELP, which is specific to the transaction you are using. This can also be accessed through the help button ⑨ or through keyboard shortcut ⌈F1⌉. This can be especially helpful if you are unsure what a specific field means or what a transaction does. This is typically provided by SAP, but your system administrator can add information to the help text to customize it to your organization if needed. The HELP menu can also take you to the SAP LIBRARY or to the GLOSSARY. These options will open a new Internet browser window to SAP's help pages online.

Help for information messages

As you work in an SAP system, you'll frequently see information, warning, or error messages. For additional help or information on the message, you can typically double click on the message, or click on the question mark symbol.

F1 help

Pressing F1 (or clicking the ⑳ button) can give you useful information from almost anywhere in an SAP system. As you scroll through the SAP menu, you can select a menu item and press F1 for information on that area or transaction. You can also click on fields (blank or field names) in nearly any transaction, press F1, and view definitions or information about that field. In some cases, the help window will also link to additional information.

In the upper left corner of your SAP screen, you'll see a small button that looks like a square with a trapezoid ☞. This button will open the system menu, as shown in Figure 2.4. You can also access this menu with the keyboard shortcut Alt + ⬚. The top section of this menu gives you options for sizing your SAP window on your computer desktop.

The next section will let you close your current window, without the system prompting you to save or log off. Next, you can select CREATE SESSION to open a new session (as discussed earlier in this chapter).

The last selection is STOP TRANSACTION. This option is particularly useful if you have a long running transaction or report, and you want to cancel it before it finishes or times out. Simply click this option, and your transaction will stop and you'll return to the SAP menu.

Another option to stop a transaction

 Another way to stop a long-running transaction is in your Windows task bar. In your task bar, find the SAP session with the transaction you want to cancel. Right click on that session and the system menu appears (as shown in Figure 2.5). Select STOP TRANSACTION to cancel your transaction.

Figure 2.4: System menu

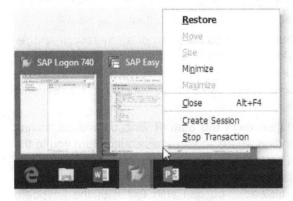

Figure 2.5: System menu by right clicking in Windows taskbar

2.1.2 System function bar

The SYSTEM FUNCTION BAR is below the MENU BAR (see Figure 2.1). It holds a variety of buttons to help navigate and quickly perform certain functions. Each button is described below. Sometimes certain buttons will be unavailable to use—in that case they will appear greyed-out or monochrome, and won't do anything when you click on them.

▶ ENTER ✅: This button can confirm and validate what you've entered or selected in your SAP screen. It does not save your work. If you seem to be stuck in a screen and unable to navigate to other fields or transactions, try clicking this button to see if it helps—sometimes you need it to validate your entries before moving on. You can also do this by hitting Enter on your keyboard.

▶ COMMAND FIELD ⬚: Here is where you enter transaction codes. Clicking the triangle on the right side of the field will bring up your recent transaction history, allowing you to choose a recently entered transaction code. If this field is not showing on your screen, click the OPEN COMMAND FIELD button ▷ to open it. If you don't want to see the COMMAND FIELD, click the same button to close it.

▶ SAVE 💾: This button saves your work. Depending on the screen or transaction, this may save and post a document or save a selection variant. You can also save by using keyboard shortcut Ctrl + S, or sometimes through the menu EDIT • SAVE.

▶ BACK ⬅: This button lets you back out of a transaction and return to the previous screen without saving your work. If your screen has required fields, you may need to complete those before using this button. You can also go back by using keyboard shortcut F3.

▶ EXIT 🔙: This button exits the current function without saving your work. Depending where you are, this could return you to the initial transaction screen, to the main menu screen, or log you off of the system. If the BACK button isn't working for you, try using the EXIT button instead. You can also exit with the keyboard shortcut ⇧ + F3.

▶ CANCEL ❌: This button will exit the current task without saving your work. Access this function with keyboard shortcut F12.

▶ PRINT 🖨: Use this button when you want to print something from your current screen. This will often give you a preview of what will print out, which can be quite helpful. You can use keyboard shortcut [Ctrl] + [P] to access this function.

▶ FIND 🏛 and FIND NEXT 🏛: Use these buttons when you are looking for a specific string of text or characters in a screen or report. FIND ([Ctrl] + [F]) will find the next occurrence, and Find Next ([Ctrl] + [G]) can find the next or multiple occurrences.

Wildcard searches

 If required, you can use wildcards when you are searching for something. Using '+' in your search will find any single character, while using '*' in your search will find any set of characters.

▶ Navigation buttons:

These next four buttons will help you move up and down through long reports or screens.

▶ FIRST PAGE 🗐: Use this button (or shortcut [Ctrl] + [PgUp]) to go to the beginning or first page of data.

▶ PREVIOUS PAGE 🗐: Use this button (or shortcut [PgUp]) to go up one page in your screen.

▶ NEXT PAGE 🗐: Use this button (or shortcut [PgDn]) to go down one page in your screen.

▶ LAST PAGE 🗐 : Use this button (or shortcut [Ctrl] + [PgDn]) to go to the end or last page of data.

▶ CREATE SESSION 🗒:

As discussed in Section 2.1.1, you can use this button to create a new session to allow multi-tasking.

▶ GENERATES SHORTCUT 🗗:

Use this button to create a desktop shortcut to a specific transaction.

Desktop transaction shortcut

 Is there a specific transaction that you use frequently? For example, do you need to complete a timesheet every day in transaction CAT2? If so, use this button to create a desktop shortcut. This will let you go directly to that transaction, saving you a few keyboard strokes or mouse clicks. If you are already logged into SAP, your shortcut transaction will open in a new session. If you aren't yet logged in, the shortcut will take you to the login screen, then to your transaction. You can also create a desktop shortcut by right clicking the transaction in the SAP menu, and choosing CREATE SHORTCUT ON THE DESKTOP, as shown in Figure 2.6.

▼ ⊟ Time Sheet
   ▼ ⊟ CATS Classic
      · ⊗ CAT3 - Display Working Times
      · ⊗ CAT2 - Record Working Times

   ▶ ☐ CATS for Service Providers   **Execute: Record Working Times**
   ▶ ☐ Approval   E̲xecute in new window
   ▶ ☐ Information System   D̲isplay documentation
   ▶ ☐ Transfer
   ▶ ☐ Tools   A̲dd to Favorites
☐ Payroll   C̲reate shortcut on the desktop
☐ Training and Event Management

Figure 2.6: Context menu to create a desktop shortcut for an SAP transaction

▶ HELP ⑦ : As discussed in Section 2.1.1, this button will let you access SAP help for the transaction, field, or screen you are using.

▶ CUSTOMIZE LOCAL LAYOUT ▦ : This button allows you to customize your display, as discussed in Section 1.2.

Hardcopy

 If you need a printed screen shot of your SAP screen, you can use the CUSTOMIZE LOCAL LAYOUT button, then choose HARDCOPY. This will print a copy of your screen to your default printer.

Command field entries

You can use the command field to enter *transaction codes*, or t-codes, rather than using the menu path. A transaction code is an alpha-numeric shortcut to access a particular function or program. In the SAP menu section, I'll go into more detail on how to find a transaction code.

In many cases, a transaction code is 4 characters long, ending in a number. That number can give you a clue as to what the transaction does. As a general rule, transactions ending in 1 are used to create something, transactions ending in 2 are used to change something, and transactions ending in 3 are used to display something. For example, when you are working with material master data, you would use transaction MM01 to create a new material, MM02 to change the material, or MM03 to display the material.

The first letter of a transaction code also gives you a clue as to what the transaction does. For example, transactions starting with M are all related to material management. However, not all of them are so easy to figure out. SAP was developed in Germany, so many of the transactions are based on the German language. Figure 2.7 shows a few of the possible starting letters for transaction codes and the name of the corresponding module in both German and English.

Transaction code first letter	Function (module) in German	Function (module) in English
A	Anlagenbuchhaltung	Asset Accounting
F	Finanzbuchhaltung	Financial Accounting
I	Instandhaltung	Plant Maintenance
K	Kostenrechung	Controlling
L	Lagerwirtschaft	Warehouse Management
M	Materialwirtschaft	Materials Management
P	Personalwesen	Human Resources
V	Vertrieb	Sales

Figure 2.7: Transaction code starting letters with modules in German and English

Z* transactions

 You may run into transactions that start with the letter Z. This typically indicates that it is a custom transaction. That means that it was not delivered by SAP, but developed internally by one of your programmers.

Transaction history

 Your command field will also maintain history of the last several transaction codes you've entered. This can be very useful when you're running reports or transactions with particularly long transaction codes. Click on the down arrow button in the command field to display the most recently used transactions, as shown in Figure 2.8.

Figure 2.8: Transaction history in the command field

Along with the typical transaction codes that will take you from the SAP Easy Access screen to a business transaction, there are several other tips for using this field to manage your SAP sessions. Here are some of those tips:

▶ /Nxxxx or /*xxxx (xxxx = a transaction code): Use this to navigate to a new transaction directly from your existing transaction without having to return to the main menu screen. For example, if you are using transaction MM03 and want to create a production order, you can enter /NC001 to go directly to the create production order transaction.

▶ /Oxxxx (xxxx = a transaction code): Similar to /N, you can use this to navigate to a new transaction without returning to the main menu. /O will open the new transaction in another session. For example, from transaction MM03, you can enter /OC001 to open the create production order transaction in another session, while leaving MM03 open in your first session.

▶ /N: Entering /N without a transaction will take you directly to the main menu screen in your current session (without saving data from your transaction).

▶ /I: Entering /I will close your current session (without saving), while leaving all other sessions open.

▶ /O: Entering /O will display a session list (see Figure 2.9), and let you create a new session, or delete one of those sessions.

▶ /NEND: Entering /NEND will let you log off and exit all of your open sessions, with a prompt to save data before exiting (see Figure 2.10).

▶ /NEX: Entering /NEX will let you log off and exit all of your open sessions, **without** a prompt to save data before exiting.

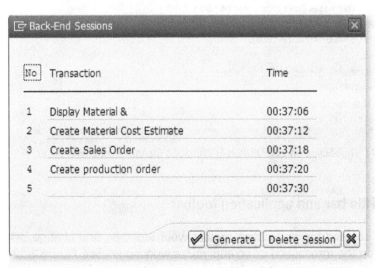

Figure 2.9: Session list displayed with command /O

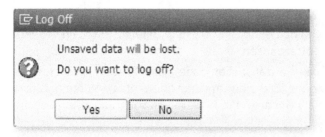

Figure 2.10: Prompt to save data with command /NEND

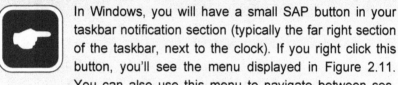

Use the Windows taskbar to manage SAP sessions

In Windows, you will have a small SAP button in your taskbar notification section (typically the far right section of the taskbar, next to the clock). If you right click this button, you'll see the menu displayed in Figure 2.11. You can also use this menu to navigate between sessions, close certain sessions, or quickly shut down SAP.

Figure 2.11: Right click on SAP button in Windows taskbar notification area

2.1.3 Title bar and application toolbar

The title bar and the application toolbar work together, and change depending on the transaction or screen you're working in. See Figure 2.12, Figure 2.13, and Figure 2.14 for examples of how these two toolbars change for different transactions.

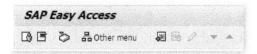

Figure 2.12: Title and application toolbar for SAP Easy Access (main menu)

Figure 2.13: Title and application toolbar for transaction MM03 (display material master)

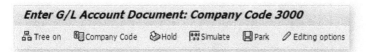

Figure 2.14: Title and application toolbar for transaction FB50 (enter G/L account document)

To get more information about what a particular button does, you can hover your mouse over the button to see a short description.

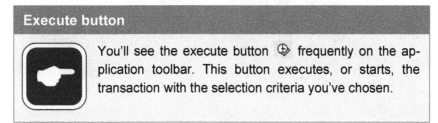

Execute button

You'll see the execute button ⊕ frequently on the application toolbar. This button executes, or starts, the transaction with the selection criteria you've chosen.

2.1.4 Dynpro area

The dynpro area is basically the main work area of your SAP screen. This area changes depending on your activities. Figure 2.15 shows the dynpro area from your main menu screen (SAP Easy Access), where you can navigate through the menu path to find transactions. Figure 2.16 shows the dynpro area from transaction MM02, where you can change and update various fields in the material master.

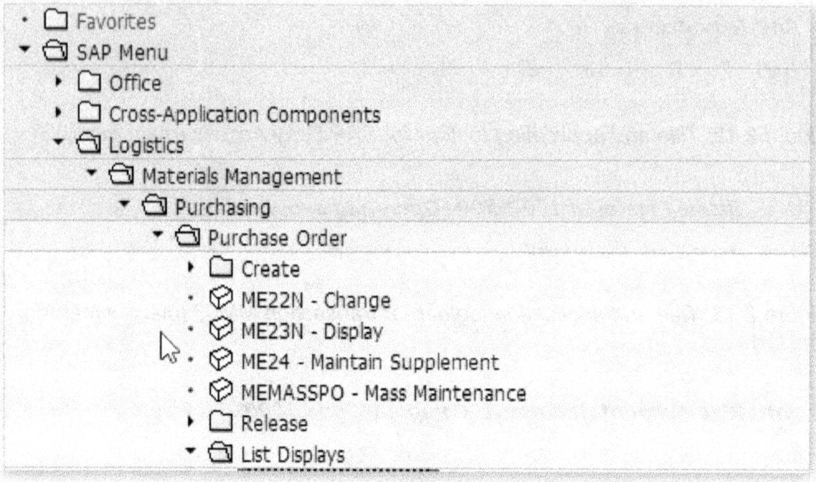

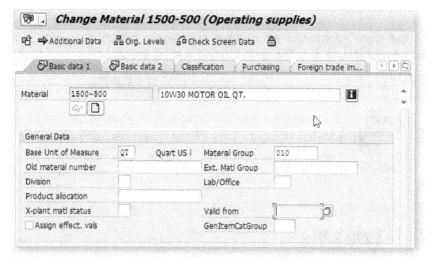

Figure 2.15: Dynpro area for SAP Easy Access (main menu)

Figure 2.16: Dynpro area for transaction MM02 (change material master)

Below are descriptions of some of the elements you'll see in the dynpro area, and how to use them.

SAP menu

When you first log into SAP, you will see SAP EASY ACCESS and the SAP menu (see Figure 2.15). The menu is organized by module and can help you navigate and find nearly any transaction you ever need to use. To open or close a node on the menu path, you can either double click on the caption or click the small triangle to the left of the caption. When you get to a transaction, or a level with a dot instead of a triangle (see ME22N—CHANGE in Figure 2.15), you can double click on that transaction, or click it and use the ENTER button.

Navigating the menu path

 While it can take a few extra mouse clicks to navigate the menu path, doing so can be a great way to find new transactions and functionality.

By default, your SAP menu will probably show the transaction description, but not the transaction code. You can view the transaction code by following the menu path EXTRAS • TECHNICAL DETAILS (see Figure 2.17). That will bring up the DISPLAY TECHNICAL DETAILS window, as shown in Figure 2.18. In this window, you can see the transaction code, the transaction text (description of the transaction), and the *area menu*.

Extras	System	Help	
Administration information		Ctrl+Shift+F8	
Assign users			
Display documentation		Shift+F6	
Technical details		Shift+F11	
Settings		Shift+F9	
Set start transaction		Shift+F7	

Figure 2.17: Technical details menu path

Display Technical Details	
Transaction Code	ME22N
Transaction text	Change Purchase Order
Area menu	ME00

Figure 2.18: Display technical details window

Area menu

 Area menus can narrow down the SAP menu to a more concentrated area. If you know your area menu, you can enter that code in the command field, like any other transaction code, and it will show you a limited menu, including the relevant transactions. For example, if you enter ME00 (from Figure 2.18) in the command field, you'll see the area menu for purchasing, showing you a focused menu for purchasing transactions (see Figure 2.19). A short list of available area menus is shown in Figure 2.20. More of these can be found in transaction SE43, or developed by your system administrator.

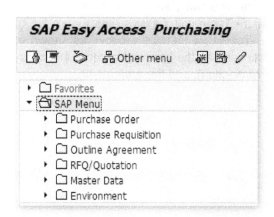

Figure 2.19: Area menu for purchasing (transaction ME00)

To see the transaction code in your SAP menu, go to the MENU BAR, and go to EXTRAS • SETTINGS (or ⌂ + F9). Check the box next to DISPLAY TECHNICAL NAMES as shown in Figure 2.21. In Figure 2.22, you can see how the menu path looks without this field selected, with the transaction description. Then, in Figure 2.23, you can see how it looks when you select the option to display technical names. The transaction code is displayed along with the transaction description.

Area Menu t-code	Area Menu
C000	Overhead cost controlling information system
CO00	Shop floor control
CPRO	Project management
F000	Financial accounting information system
FIAA	Asset accounting information system
FIAP	Reports for accounts payable accounting
FIAR	Reports for accounts receivable accounting
IF00	Production resources/tools
IW00	Maintenance processing
KEMN	Profitability analysis
MB00	Inventory management
MC00	Logistics Information System (LIS)
ME00	Purchasing
MM00	Material master
PA00	Personnel administration
QA00	Quality inspection
QE00	Quality planning
VA00	Sales
VF00	Billing

Figure 2.20: Selection of area menu transactions

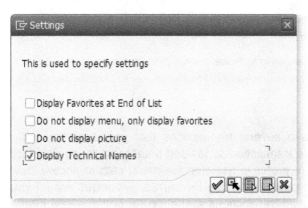

Figure 2.21: Displaying technical names (transaction codes) in SAP menu

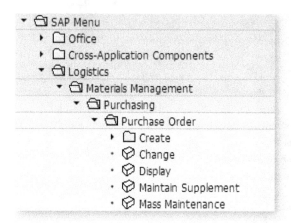

Figure 2.22: Menu path without showing technical names (transaction codes)

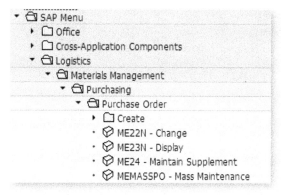

Figure 2.23: Menu path showing technical names (transaction codes)

Favorites

You will probably have several transactions that you use repeatedly. Some users memorize transaction codes and enter them manually every time, while other users prefer to navigate the menu path to access their transactions. Another option is to use FAVORITES. FAVORITES will let you organize your most-used transactions at the top (or bottom—see Figure 2.21) of the SAP menu so that they are easily accessed. If you have lots of favorite transactions, you can also organize them into folders.

If you already know the transaction you want to add to your favorites, use the MENU BAR path FAVORITES • INSERT TRANSACTION (Ctrl + ⬦ + F4). Enter the transaction code in the box (see Figure 2.24), then it will be added to your favorites.

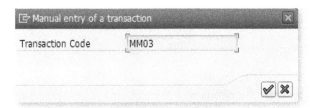

Figure 2.24: Manually entering a transaction in Favorites

If you're not sure of the transaction code, you can also navigate the menu path to find your transaction. Once you've found your transaction and clicked to select it, you have a couple of options. You can right click on the transaction, then choose ADD TO FAVORITES (see Figure 2.25). You can also click the ADD TO FAVORITES button 🔲 or use keyboard shortcut `Ctrl` + `⇧` + `F6`.

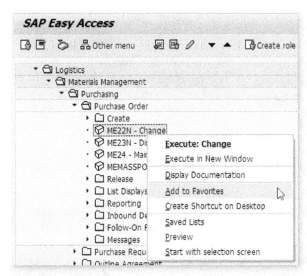

Figure 2.25: Add to Favorites by right clicking from the menu path

If you have a long list of favorite transactions, you may want to organize them into folders. For example, you could create folders to separate your favorite transactions for reporting, order creation, and master data maintenance. To create a folder, you can use the menu path FAVORITES • INSERT FOLDER (`Ctrl` + `⇧` + `F5`). In the CREATE A FOLDER box (shown in Figure 2.26), you can name your folder, then press `Enter` or click the CONTINUE button ✅ . Your new folder will show in the favorites section of the SAP menu, as shown in Figure 2.27

Figure 2.26: Create a folder in the Favorites list

Figure 2.27: Folder in the Favorites list

Right click to add a folder

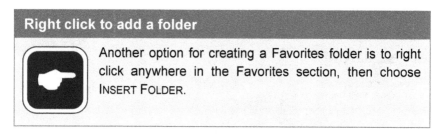

Another option for creating a Favorites folder is to right click anywhere in the Favorites section, then choose INSERT FOLDER.

Once you've created folders, you have different options for putting your favorite transactions in the folder. One option is to click on any transaction in the SAP menu (either already in your Favorites or in the main section of the menu) and drag it into your chosen folder. Release the mouse button when your cursor is over the folder name, as shown in Figure 2.28. Another option is to right click on your folder to get the context menu (see Figure 2.29), select INSERT TRANSACTION, and then enter your transaction code.

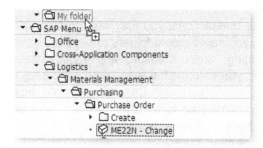

Figure 2.28: Click and drag a transaction into Favorites folder

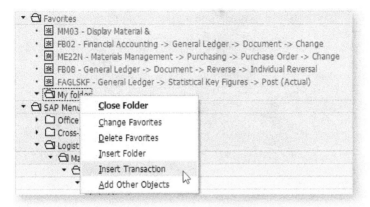

Figure 2.29: Context menu to insert transaction into Favorites folder

You can also export or import Favorites to share the same list among coworkers, rather than each person adding them manually. To export your Favorites, follow the menu path FAVORITES • DOWNLOAD TO PC. (see Figure 2.30). Save the file to your desktop, then you can share it with colleagues.

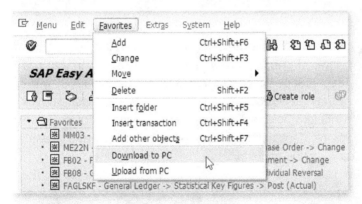

Figure 2.30: Menu path to export Favorites

Conversely, if you want to import Favorites from someone else, you can follow the menu path FAVORITES • UPLOAD FROM PC. In the OPEN window, choose the file location and click the OPEN button, as shown in Figure 2.31. The transactions will then show up in your Favorites menu.

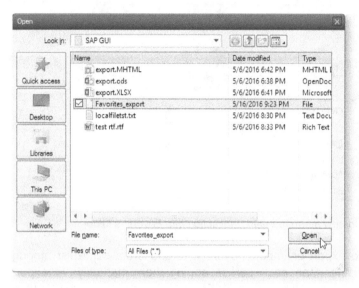

Figure 2.31: Upload Favorites: Choose file location

Context sensitive menus (right click)

 By right clicking on objects in SAP, you can get a context-sensitive menu that will give you other options, depending on where you are. In Figure 2.25, you can see options specific to transaction ME22N, including the ability to execute (run) the transaction, open a new window to execute it, display the help documentation, or create a desktop shortcut. Check out the context-sensitive menus as you work in SAP to see what you can find.

Searching the SAP menu path

 What if you know a transaction code, but you want to know the menu path to get there? Or you know part of the transaction name, but can't remember the transaction code? Maybe you want to look at related transactions in the menu path. Check out the transaction SEARCH_SAP_MENU. This transaction will let you search the entire menu and give you all of the possible menu paths for your transaction code.

Fields

Fields are where you enter data. In Figure 2.16, one example is the field BASE UNIT OF MEASURE, where the user has entered QT for quart.

Many fields will have a list of existing entries. For example, you can see the VALID FROM field in Figure 2.16 is highlighted, and has a dropdown or *matchcode* box 🔲 on the right. This will provide a search box or list of possible entries for the field. You can also access this search functionality with the F4 key.

Other fields allow you to enter your own text. The material description field shown in Figure 2.16 is an example of one of these. The user has entered 10W30 MOTOR OIL QT. here. In some text fields, you are limited to a certain number of characters. If there is a limit, the system will usually stop you from typing anything more into the field.

Radio buttons and checkboxes

In some transactions, you'll need to choose from various options. You may see radio buttons or checkboxes to make these choices. The selection screen for transaction MB5L shows both of these options (see Figure 2.32).

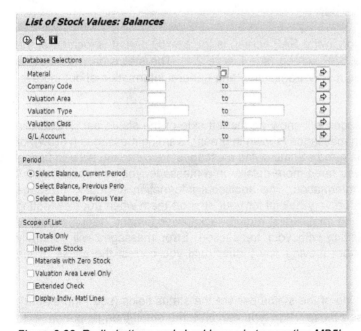

Figure 2.32: Radio buttons and checkboxes in transaction MB5L

Under PERIOD, there are radio buttons to choose the display period. Radio buttons allow you to choose only one option, so in this case we've chosen to display the current period balance.

Under SCOPE OF LIST, there are checkboxes. Checkboxes allow you to choose multiple options. In this case, for example, you could choose to view negative stocks and to display individual material lines.

Tabs

Many transactions have enormous amounts of fields and data. If all of these fields were displayed in a single screen, it would be difficult and confusing to read. Organizing these fields into tabs can categorize the information, which serves multiple purposes. Not only does it make it easier for a user to find what they are looking for, it also provides a method to limit authorization to only certain areas.

For a few examples of transactions using tabs, you can see MM03 (display material master), MIRO (enter incoming invoice), or VA03 (display sales order).

2.1.5   Status bar

The last section in the SAP screen is the STATUS BAR. It is located at the bottom of the SAP screen (see Figure 2.1). The status bar can provide messages about your transaction and general information about the system.

System messages will show on the left side of the status bar. These can be information messages (shown in green), warning messages (yellow), or error messages (red). Some of the messages are clear and easy to understand, but if you need more details on a message, you can double click it to get more information. The additional information (including message numbers) can be very helpful for your support team when troubleshooting issues. Warning messages require acknowledgement (Enter button) before proceeding with your transaction. Error messages will generally prevent you from moving any further until you correct the cause of the error.

On the right side of the status bar are the status fields (see Figure 2.33). If you don't see these fields, you can click the small triangle button ◁ to expand them.

▷ ¦ SESSION_MANAGER ▼ ¦ sap01-205 ¦ OVR ¦

Figure 2.33: Status fields

The first status field gives you a choice of what to display. You can click on the small black triangle on the right (see Figure 2.34) to choose between the following options to display:

▶ SYSTEM

▶ CLIENT

▶ USER

▶ PROGRAM

▶ TRANSACTION

▶ RESPONSE TIME (AND RELATED)

I typically like to have my status bar display the TRANSACTION, so I can tell at a glance where I am, especially when I have multiple sessions open. This can also give a clue as to where you have navigated when drilling through multiple related documents. If I'm testing different functionality and working in different systems or clients, I will change this option to display that information instead of transaction. Other users will have different preferences; choose what is most useful for you.

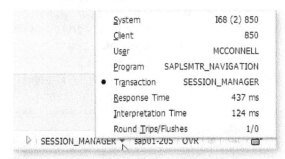

Figure 2.34: Choices for display on status bar

The next status field shows the server to which you are connected. This can also be very useful when working in multiple test or production clients (see Figure 2.35).

Figure 2.35: Server information in status bar

The last status field shows your data entry mode; either insert (INS) or overwrite (OVR). If you are in overwrite mode, then anything you enter in a field will write over and delete any existing information in that field. Insert mode will leave the existing information and insert your new entries where you have your cursor. To change this mode, you can either click in the field, or you can use the [Insert] button on your keyboard (see Figure 2.36).

SESSION_MANAGER ▼ sap01-205 [OVR]

Figure 2.36: Overwrite/insert indicator in status bar

2.2 Other navigation tips

In this section, I'll cover various tips for navigating through reports and transactions, including tips on searching, tips on selecting criteria for reports or transactions, and how to copy and paste.

2.2.1 Matchcode search tips

A matchcode search (as discussed in the Fields section) will let you search for available values for the selected field. For example, search for a material number in transaction MM03 by clicking the matchcode search button ⊡ or by pressing [F4]. In most cases, this will give you a search box where you can enter more search criteria (see Figure 2.37). Here, you can hit the [Enter] key or click the START SEARCH button ✅ to search for all available materials. If you know part of the material number or description you're searching for, you can use an asterisk * as a wild card, and enter some search criteria in the selection fields.

Maximum number of hits

As shown in Figure 2.37, the last selection is for the maximum number of hits in your search results. This typically defaults to 500, but you can increase or decrease it here. Note that a longer list of search results may take longer to run.

Looking once more at Figure 2.37, you can see a series of tabs across the top. Each of these tabs gives you different search criteria. You can navigate through the tabs by clicking the arrow buttons ◀▶ to scroll left and right, or by clicking the list button 🖳 to view the full list of available tabs.

Lastly in Figure 2.37, you'll see the MULTIPLE SELECTION button ⬖. By clicking in a field (such as material description), then clicking this button, you can search multiple strings or ranges in the material description field (see Figure 2.38).

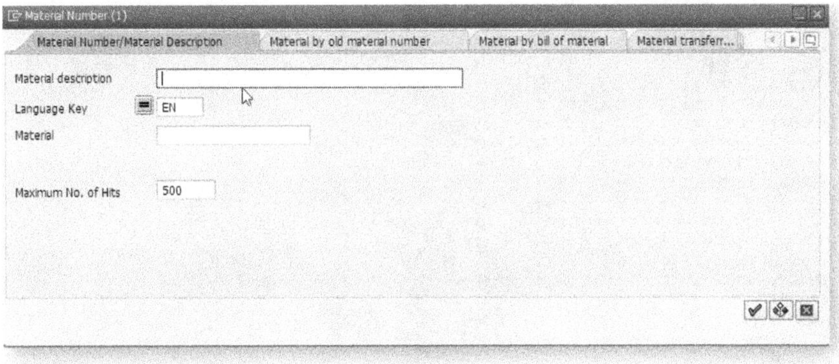

Figure 2.37: Material number search criteria

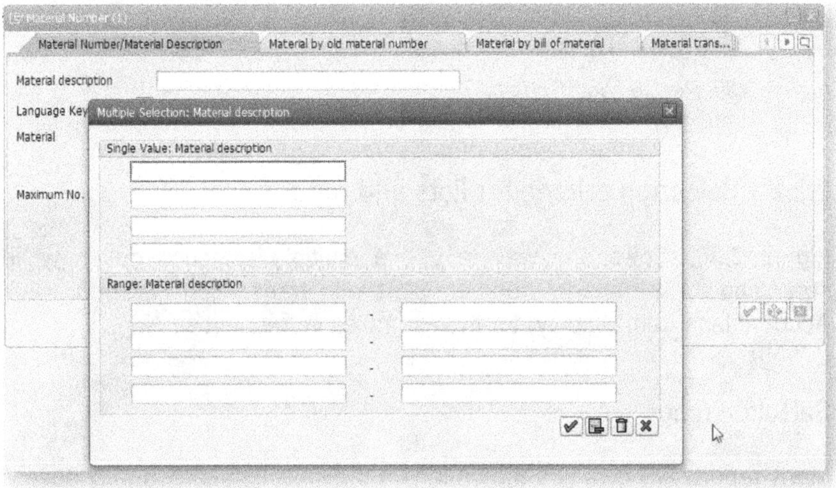

Figure 2.38: Material description multiple selection box

If you have searched for something, but you then want to revise your search criteria without exiting the search, you can click on the bar with the small down arrow to open up the search selection criteria box (see Figure 2.39).

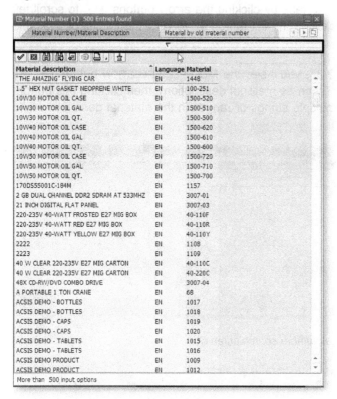

Figure 2.39: Revise search criteria

2.2.2 Selection criteria for lists and reports

Figure 2.38 shows one way to use a multiple selection option while searching for a material number. Start with transaction FAGLL03 (G/L Account Line Item Display) for the examples in the next section.

Selection range

Many reports will give you the option on the selection screen to choose a range of options (G/L account numbers in this case). In Figure 2.40, you can see that the G/L account and company code selections show two fields, separated by "to". This indicates that you can select a full range of accounts or company codes, rather than a single one. Choose the G/L account range of 10000 to 19999 to show information for every G/L account in that range.

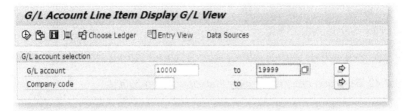

Figure 2.40: Select a range of G/L accounts

Selection options

The next tip for selecting report criteria is SELECTION OPTIONS. Some transactions will have a SELECTION OPTIONS button Selection Options, but you can also access these options by double clicking on your selection field. In Figure 2.41, you can see the SELECTION OPTIONS window, obtained by double clicking on the G/L account field. This window gives you the option to use relational operators, such as greater than or less than signs, to choose your accounts. When you select one of these operators, it will show on your main selection screen, as shown in Figure 2.42. This selection will show data for every G/L account starting with account 50000.

Figure 2.41: Selection options window

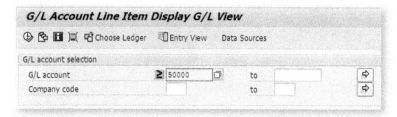

Figure 2.42: Selection options: Greater than or equal to 50000

The SELECTION OPTIONS window also has a button [⚙ Exclude from Selection] to exclude certain items from your selection criteria. If you click this, then the operators will turn red to indicate that you are excluding that criterion, not including it (see Figure 2.43). In Figure 2.44, you can see a red equal sign, indicating that the selection will exclude everything except the accounts from 50000 to 59999.

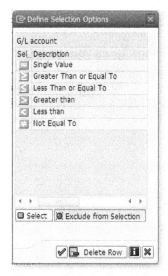

Figure 2.43: Selection options: Exclude from selection

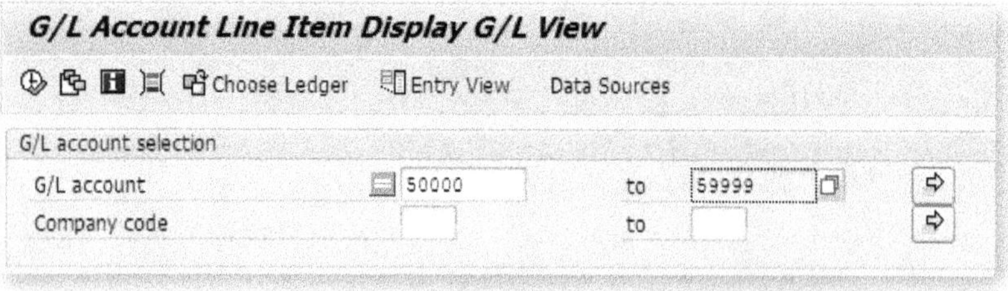

Figure 2.44: Selection options: Exclude accounts from 50000 to 59999

Multiple selection

Another feature on many selection screens is the MULTIPLE SELECTION button ⮕. Clicking this button will bring up a multiple selection window (shown in Figure 2.45). This window has tabs to select a list of single values, a list of ranges, or exclude lists of single values or ranges.

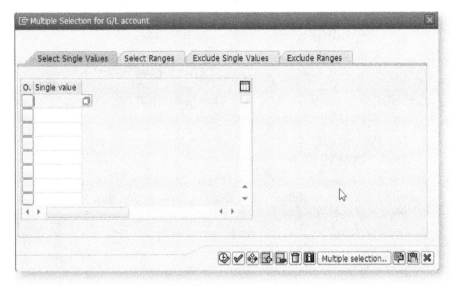

Figure 2.45: Multiple selection window for G/L account

Figure 2.46: Buttons in multiple selection window

The row of buttons along the bottom of the window provides some additional selection options and functionality (see Figure 2.46). Here are the functions of each of the buttons:

1. COPY (keyboard shortcut F8): Click this button when you're finished making selections in this window. This will copy your multiple selection criteria to the main selection screen.

2. CHECK ENTRIES (Enter): This button will check for any errors in your entries.

3. DEFINE SELECTION OPTIONS (F2): This will bring up the selection options window shown in Figure 2.41. You can also view selection options by clicking the OPTIONS PUSHBUTTON on a line .

4. INSERT LINE (⬙ + F1): Click this to insert a new line into your selection list.

5. DELETE SELECTION ROW (⬙ + F2): Click on an unwanted line item in the list, then click this button to delete that line.

6. DELETE ENTIRE SELECTION (⬙ + F4): Click this button to delete all of the selection criteria in this window.

7. HELP ON SCREEN (⬙ + F6): This button will open a help window with information on using the multiple selection window.

8. MULTIPLE SELECTION (F6): Click this to open a search box where you can search for additional selections.

9. IMPORT FROM TEXT FILE (⬙ + F11): This button gives you the option to save a list of items in a text file, then import that file to use as the list of values here.

10. UPLOAD FROM CLIPBOARD (⬙ + F12): You can copy a list of values from elsewhere (such as a spreadsheet or a report in SAP), then copy it into the list of values here.

11. CANCEL (F12): Click this button to cancel your multiple selection activity and return to the main selection screen.

Additional selections

Some transactions offer more selection criteria than what you see on the initial selection screen. Here are some ways that you can find additional selection criteria:

▶ CUSTOM SELECTIONS)≣((Ctrl + F1): This button will open up a FREE SELECTION screen. In the G/L example, free selections will let you choose G/L line items by all sorts of criteria available in a financial document. As shown in Figure 2.47, the available fields are shown in a frame on the left side. Double click on the fields you want to select by, and those will show as DYNAMIC SE-LECTIONS in the larger frame on the right.

▶ ALL SELECTIONS 🄳 (⎡⇧⎤ + ⎡F7⎤): This button will expand the selection screen to show additional selection criteria. A good example of this is found in transaction S_P99_41000111 (Analyze/Compare Material Cost Estimates). Figure 2.48 shows the initial selection screen, with a few fields available for selection. When you click on the ALL SELECTIONS button 🄳, it expands the selection screen to show all available fields (as shown in Figure 2.49).

▶ CHOOSE... Choose... (⎡Ctrl⎤ + ⎡F1⎤): One example of this button is seen in transaction ME2L (Purchasing Documents per Vendor) and other similar purchasing document list display transactions. Figure 2.50 shows the window where you can choose exactly which types of purchasing documents you want to display.

▶ FURTHER SEL.CRITERIA Further sel.criteria (⎡⇧⎤ + ⎡F8⎤): Figure 2.51 shows this button used in transaction VA05 List of Sales Orders. Clicking this button allows you to view a list of sales orders selected by more criteria not available on the initial selection screen.

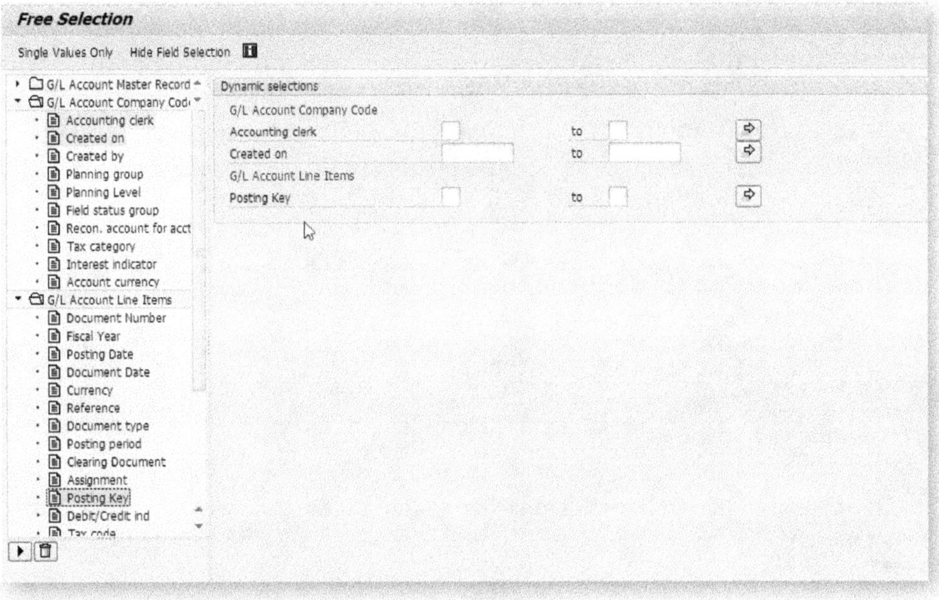

Figure 2.47: Free selection screen for FAGLL03

Analyze/Compare Material Cost Estimates

⊕ Selection Options 🐂 🖅 🖶 🖩 🏛 Comparison Value...

Selection

Plant	[ ] 🗗		⇨
Material Number		to	⇨
Costing Variant			⇨
Costing Version			⇨
Costing Date, Valid From			⇨

Output

Cost Component View	1	Cost of goods manufactured

Figure 2.48: Initial selection screen for analyze/compare material cost estimates

Analyze/Compare Material Cost Estimates

⊕ Selection Options 🐂 🖅 🖶 🖩 🏛 Comparison Value...

Selection

	Costing Run 1	Costing Run 2	
Costing Run			
Costing Date			
☑ Intersection of Runs 1 and 2			
Plant	[ ] 🗗		⇨
Material Number		to	⇨
Costing Variant			⇨
Costing Version			⇨
Costing Date, Valid From			⇨
Costing Status			⇨
Costing Level		to	⇨
☐ No Material Components			

Exceptions

Comparison Value		< no comparison value >
Threshold Red [Amount]		[%]
Threshold Yellow [Amount]		[%]
☑ Display Positive and Negative Variances		
☑ Only Display Exceptions		

Output

Material Master Price	1	Standard price
Layout		

Figure 2.49: All selections (expanded) for analyze/compare material cost estimates

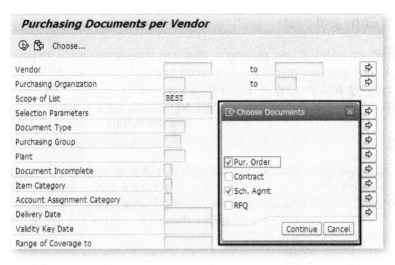

Figure 2.50: Choose documents in purchasing document list display

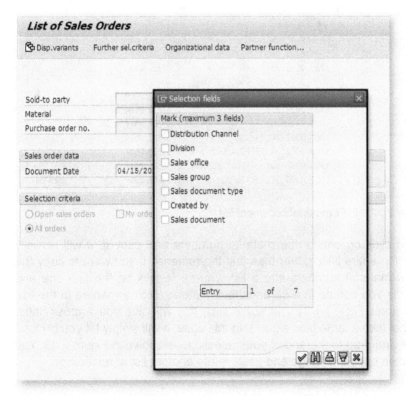

Figure 2.51: Further selection criteria in VA05 list of sales orders

2.2.3 Copy and paste

I touched on copying and pasting values into a selection list in the last section, but now will discuss a few more tips and tricks. As a general rule, copying and pasting in an SAP system works in much the same manner as in other applications: select something, copy it using a keyboard shortcut ([Ctrl] + [C]) or button, and paste it ([Ctrl] + [V]) elsewhere.

In an application like Microsoft Excel, you can click in a cell and drag to capture your selection (or click to select the values from a single cell), then copy. One trick to use in SAP for copying from a report or list display is [Ctrl] + [Y]. Use transaction MB51 (Material Document List) as an example (shown in Figure 2.52).

Material Document List

Material	Plant	SLoc	MvT	S	Mat. Doc. ⌃	Item	Posting Date	Qty in unit of entry	EUn
R-B411	1000	0001	261		4900008172	4	06/21/2014	1-	PC
R-T411	1000	0001	261		4900008173	1	06/21/2014	1-	PC
R-B311	1000	0001	101	E	4900008180	1	07/28/2014	1	PC
R-B111	1000	0001	261		4900008181	1	07/28/2014	1-	PC
R-B211	1000	0001	261			2	07/28/2014	1-	PC
R-B311	1000	0001	261	E		3	07/28/2014	1-	PC
R-B411	1000	0001	261			4	07/28/2014	1-	PC
R-F111	1000	0002	101	E	4900008182	1	07/28/2014	1	PC
DPC1003	1200	0001	601		4900008190	1	08/28/2014	10-	PC
P-100	1000	0002	561		4900008191	1	09/15/2014	1,000	PC

Figure 2.52: MB51 material document list

If you click on one of the material numbers and copy it, it will actually copy the entire line, rather than just the material. If you want to copy the first 5 material numbers into a list, you can't click on the first one and drag as you can do in a spreadsheet. Instead, click anywhere in the list, then press [Ctrl] + [Y]. In some lists, this will give you a cross-hatch symbol (like a large plus sign +). In this case, it will simply let you click on a cell and drag to the end of your selection, as shown in Figure 2.53. You can then copy this range and paste it into another list or application.

Material Document List

Material	Plant	SLoc	MvT	S	Mat. Doc.	Item	Posting Date	Qty in unit of entry	EUn
R-B411	1000	0001	261		4900008172	4	06/21/2014	1-	PC
R-T411	1000	0001	261		4900008173	1	06/21/2014	1-	PC
R-B311	1000	0001	101	E	4900008180	1	07/28/2014	1	PC
R-B111	1000	0001	261		4900008181	1	07/28/2014	1-	PC
R-B211	1000	0001	261			2	07/28/2014	1-	PC
R-B311	1000	0001	261	E		3	07/28/2014	1-	PC
R-B411	1000	0001	261			4	07/28/2014	1-	PC
R-F111	1000	0002	101	E	4900008182	1	07/28/2014	1	PC
DPC1003	1200	0001	601		4900008190	1	08/28/2014	10-	PC

Figure 2.53: MB51 document list with range selected with Ctrl + Y

Copying in configuration screens

The IMG (implementation guide), or configuration, has some additional options for copying pieces of a configuration. For example, if you are configuring a new company, you can copy and edit an existing company, rather than creating it completely from scratch. You can select a single line to copy (see Figure 2.54), or you can use the SELECT ALL button 🔳 or the SELECT BLOCK button 🔳 to select multiple lines to copy. Click the copy button 🔳 to copy and edit that entry to quickly create a new company.

Change View "Internal trading partners": Overview

New Entries

Company	Company name	Name of company 2
1	Gesellschaft G00000	
5	IDES NGL AG	
6	IDES US	
7	IDES NGL AG	
1000	IDES AG	
1002	Singapore Company	
2000	IDES UK LTD	
2100	IDES Portugal	
2200	IDES France	
2201	IDES France affiliate	
2300	IDES España	
2400	IDES Filiale1 IT Ko.1000	
2500	IDES Netherlands	
2600	IDES Italia	
2700	IDES Schweiz	
3000	IDES US INC	

Figure 2.54: IMG create company configuration: Select entry to copy

2.3 Review and quick reference

Chapter 2 covered many tips and tricks for navigating SAP. You looked at the different sections of an SAP screen and what they do, and looked at each of the buttons on the SYSTEM FUNCTION BAR (see the quick reference table in Figure 2.55). You also reviewed how to use matchcode searches to look for field values, how to use multiple selections for reports, and how to copy and paste from an SAP list or into a selection list. Figure 2.56 has a list of the shortcut transactions you can use to manage different work sessions.

Button	Keyboard Shortcut	Function
⑨	F1	Help
✅	Enter	Enter: confirm & validate entries
▷		Open command field. Use this if your command field (transaction code field) isn't visible.
💾	Ctrl + S	Save
⬅	F3	Back: go back to prior screen
🔙	Shift +F3	Exit: back out of transaction, or exit the system
❌	F12	Cancel
🖨	Ctrl + P	Print
🔍	Ctrl + F	Find
🔎	Ctrl + G	Find next: Find the next entry, or find multiples
⏫	Ctrl + Page Up	First page: Go to the top of the list
🔼	Page Up	Previous page: Go up one page
🔽	Page Down	Next page: Go down one page
⏬	Ctrl + Page Down	Last page: Go to the end of the list
🖼		Create session
📄		Generates shortcut: use to create a desktop shortcut for a transaction

Figure 2.55: System function bar buttons and keyboard shortcuts

Transaction	Action
/Nxxxx or /*xxxx	Go to a transaction without saving or returning to menu
/Oxxxx	Open a transaction in a new session
/N	Return to main menu without saving
/I	Close the current session
/O	Display a session list
/NEND	Log off and end sessions with prompt to save
/NEX	Log off and end sessions without prompt to save

Figure 2.56: Transactions for managing SAP work sessions

3 Integration in SAP ERP

One of the great features of SAP ERP is the interaction between modules. Purchasing, inventory management, financials, sales, and other modules are highly integrated and work together. For example, a purchase order is tied directly to a goods receipt into inventory, which is tied directly to a vendor invoice, which is then tied to related accounting transactions. Each of these also gets information from the master records for vendors, materials, and accounts. In this section, I'll discuss some tips on how to find and navigate between related documents and master data.

3.1 Double click

One of the easiest and most common ways to get to more information is by double clicking. Depending on what transaction or screen you are in, you can double click on different fields to get more details.

Other options for more details

In some cases, you can get the same result by right clicking your mouse and clicking CHOOSE from the context menu.

Going back to the purchase order example, look at some instances of how double clicking on different fields can lead to other documents or master data. Figure 3.1 shows a purchase order with transaction ME23N. First, double click on the ❶ vendor field. This will take you to the vendor master display (transaction MK03), as shown in Figure 3.2, where you can find additional information on the vendor. Click the back button ❻ or F3 to get back to the purchase order. Next, from the purchase order display, you can double click on the ❷ material number. This will take you to the purchasing view of the material master (transaction MM03), shown in Figure 3.3, where you can navigate through all of the other existing material master views. From the purchase order display, you can also click (double clicking not necessary here) on a ❸ document number in the PURCHASE ORDER HISTORY tab to view a material document (Figure 3.4) or invoice.

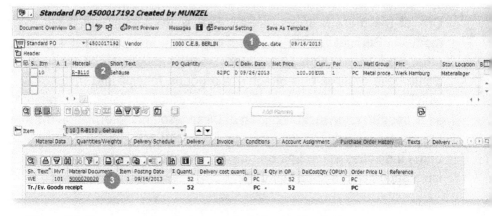

Figure 3.1: Purchase order display—navigate by double clicking

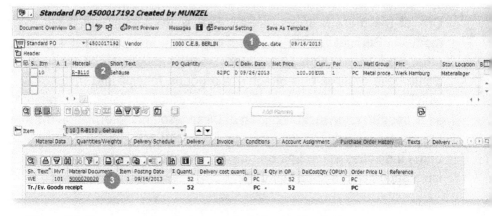

Figure 3.2: Vendor master display by double clicking in purchase order

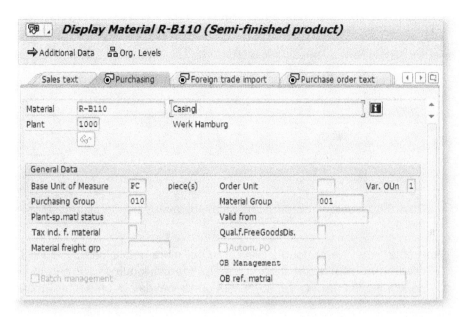

Figure 3.3: Material master display by double clicking in purchase order

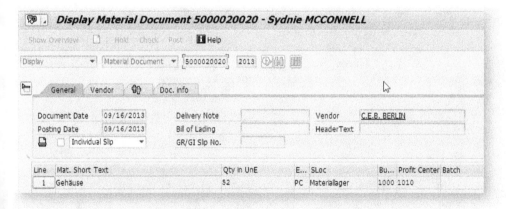

Figure 3.4: Material document display by clicking in purchase order

Displaying an accounting document from the material document

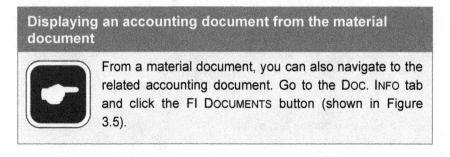 From a material document, you can also navigate to the related accounting document. Go to the Doc. Info tab and click the FI Documents button (shown in Figure 3.5).

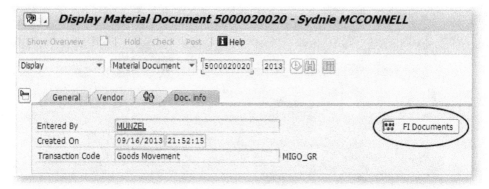

Figure 3.5: Navigate to the financials documents from a material document display

Another example of double clicking to get more details can be found in sales order display (transaction VA03). You can double click on any of the line items (see Figure 3.6) to get additional details on each of those line items. You could also double click on fields such as SOLD-TO PARTY or PO NUMBER to get additional document header details.

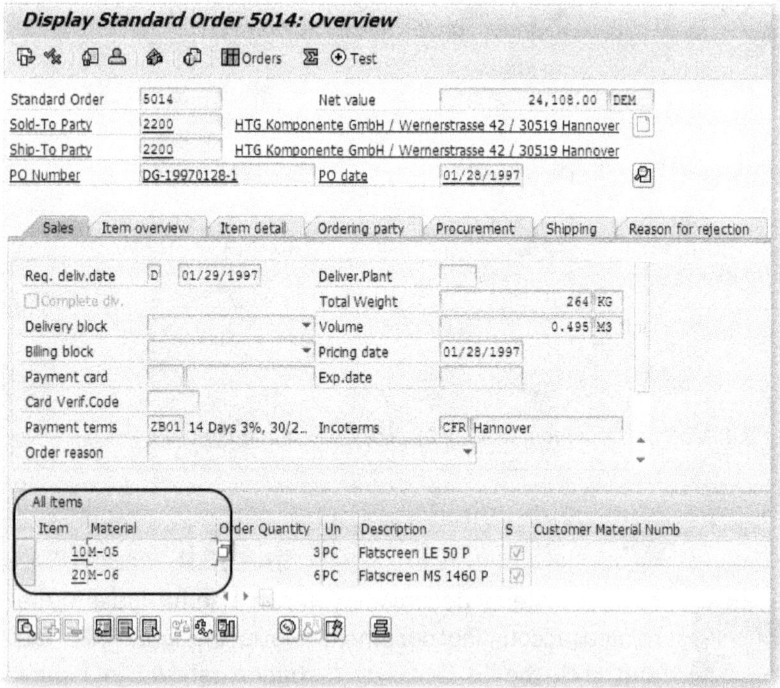

Figure 3.6: Sales order line item detail

Try it out

As you go through your work, try double clicking on various fields and see what you find.

Financial accounting document details

Depending on your version, double clicking on a financial accounting line item may not take you to the actual document. Instead, it will give you a new window with some of the document details. In that case, you can click on the DISPLAY DOCUMENT button 👓 to take you to the document.

3.2 Document flow

Document flow is a highly useful tool for navigating through sales-related documents and postings. You can access document flow from transactions such as sales orders, deliveries, or customer invoices.

Accessing document flow

In most cases, you can access document flow by going to menu path ENVIRONMENT • DISPLAY DOCUMENT FLOW, or by clicking the DISPLAY DOCUMENT FLOW button 🗗 .

Look at an example of document flow, starting in sales order display (transaction VA03), shown in Figure 3.7. On the application toolbar you'll find the display DOCUMENT FLOW BUTTON 🗗. You can find this from the sales order header, or from the line item detail display.

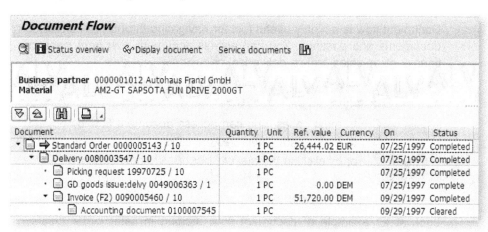

Display Standard Order 5143: Overview

Standard Order	5143		Net value	51,720.00	DEM
Sold-To Party	1012	Autohaus Franzl GmbH / Schwarzhauptstrasse 51 / 80939 Mue...			
Ship-To Party	1012	Autohaus Franzl GmbH / Schwarzhauptstrasse 51 / 80939 Mue...			
PO Number	11544445		PO date		

Figure 3.7: Display document flow button in VA03 sales order display

The document flow screen shows you a hierarchical list of documents related to the sales order (see Figure 3.8). This screen alone can give you lots of information about where this order is in the order-to-cash process, such as whether the order has been shipped or invoiced to the customer, the quantities and values of the sale, transaction dates, and statuses. For more information, you can click on an individual document then click the DETAILS button 🔍, or double click on the document. This will give you a table at the bottom of your screen with some additional details on that document (Figure 3.9). Then, you can click the DISPLAY DOCUMENT button 👓Display document to navigate directly to the linked document (shown in Figure 3.10).

Document Flow

🔍 📋 Status overview   👓Display document   Service documents 📖

Business partner 0000001012 Autohaus Franzl GmbH
Material   AM2-GT SAPSOTA FUN DRIVE 2000GT

Document	Quantity	Unit	Ref. value	Currency	On	Status
▾ 🗋 ➡ Standard Order 0000005143 / 10	1 PC		26,444.02	EUR	07/25/1997	Completed
▾ 🗋 Delivery 0080003547 / 10	1 PC				07/25/1997	Completed
· 🗋 Picking request 19970725 / 10	1 PC				07/25/1997	Completed
· 🗋 GD goods issue:delvy 0049006363 / 1	1 PC		0.00	DEM	07/25/1997	complete
▾ 🗋 Invoice (F2) 0090005460 / 10	1 PC		51,720.00	DEM	09/29/1997	Completed
· 🗋 Accounting document 0100007545	1 PC				09/29/1997	Cleared

Figure 3.8: Sales order document flow

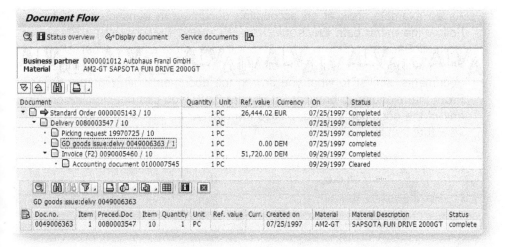

Figure 3.9: Document flow details

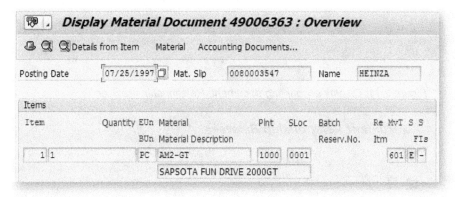

Figure 3.10: Document flow: Display document

3.3   Relationship browser

Relationship browser works similarly to document flow, but for financial documents. This can help analyze business activity from an accounting point of view.

As an example, look at an accounting document in transaction FB03. Follow the menu path ENVIRONMENT • DOCUMENT ENVIRONMENT • RELATIONSHIP BROWSER (Figure 3.11). This will take you to a hierarchical list of all related documents, including all of the linked accounting and financial documents, similar to what you saw in the document flow (Figure 3.8). From the relationship browser list (Figure 3.12), you can double click on any of the documents listed, or use the DISPLAY DOCUMENT button 🔍 to view that transaction.

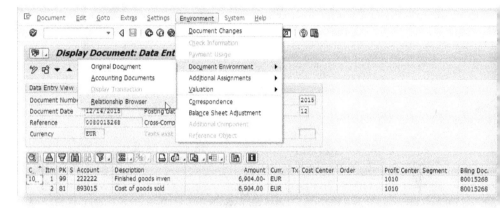

Figure 3.11: Display accounting document: Relationship browser

Document Relationship Browser

🔍

Relationship Tree	Descriptn
▼ Accounting document	1000 4900000024 2015
▼ Material Document	4900008270 2015
▶ Outbound Delivery	0080015268
• Special Ledger Document	1000 1000337910 2015 S 0F
• Controlling Document	1000 0200158233
• Profit Center Doc.	1000 0000330453 2015 A
• Special Ledger Document	1000 1000337910 2015 S BW
• Special Ledger Document	1000 1000337910 2015 S U1

Figure 3.12: Document relationship browser

Original document and accounting documents

 In Figure 3.11, the DOCUMENT ENVIRONMENT menu also has selections for original document and accounting documents. These can be used as shortcuts to get directly to those transactions, rather than viewing all available documents in RELATIONSHIP BROWSER.

3.4   Review

Chapter 3 discussed multiple ways that SAP ERP is integrated, and how a purchase order can be tied to an inventory receipt, payment, and accounting entries. You looked at how you can navigate through those linked documents by drilling through them, using document flow, or viewing the relationship browser. Another trick in this chapter was how you can often double click on an item to get additional details, such as master data or a related transaction.

4 Layouts and variants

You may have noticed that SAP ERP can not only provide a vast amount of information, but it can also ask you for a lot of information. Selection variants can help simplify the task of entering criteria on a selection screen. Layouts can let you display a personalized version of a report. I'll discuss both of these personalization options in this chapter.

4.1 Selection variants

Let's say that you frequently review purchase orders with transaction ME2L (Purchasing Documents per Vendor). Every week, you review a group of materials and their open purchase orders in your plant. As shown in Figure 4.1, this selection screen has many different fields available to help you choose exactly what you'll see in your report. For a new user or new transaction, this can be highly confusing. For an experienced or frequent user, it can be time-consuming and inefficient to enter the same criteria every time you run a report. This is where a *selection variant* can come in handy. Some selection variants are delivered (created by SAP), based on common scenarios, but you can also create variants specific to your need.

Modifying a delivered variant

Sometimes it's quick and easy to take one of the delivered variants and make a couple of changes instead of creating your own from scratch. If you do this, try saving your new variant with its own unique name. Then you can keep the delivered variants and provide a more descriptive name to make it easier for you to choose the variant you want.

4.1.1 Creating a selection variant

First, look at how to create a selection variant. In this example you'll create variants for transaction ME2L (Purchasing Documents per Vendor).

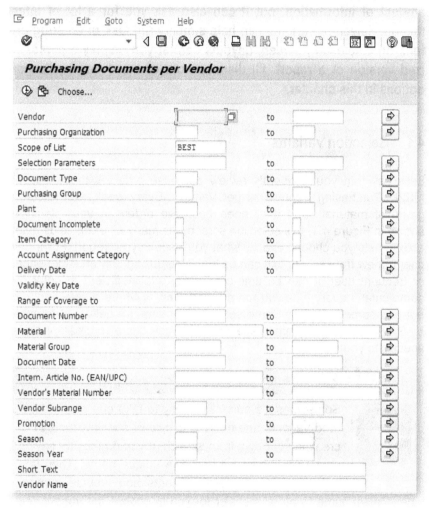

Figure 4.1: Example selection screen: Transaction ME2L (Purchasing Documents per Vendor)

To save a selection variant, start by entering your criteria in the selection screen. Figure 4.2 shows the purchasing organization, scope of list, purchasing group, and dates. Next, go to the menu path GOTO • VARIANTS • SAVE AS VARIANT. Here, give the variant a name and description, then save (Figure 4.3).

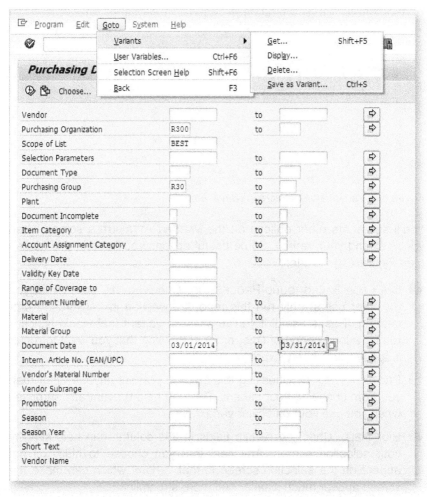

Figure 4.2: Menu path to save selection variant

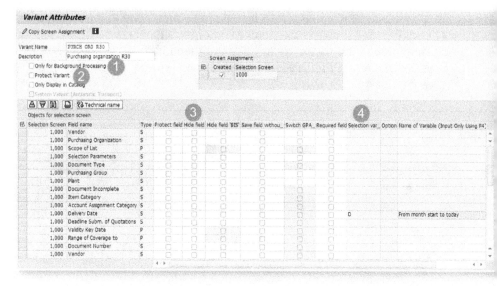

Figure 4.3: Variant attribute screen (Save variant)

You'll see some other options on the VARIANT ATTRIBUTES screen when you're saving your variant. Some useful options you'll see in this screen (see Figure 4.3) include:

❶ ONLY FOR BACKGROUND PROCESSING: Checking this box will let you (or other users) only run this report/transaction in background processing. This is useful if you've saved a variant that would typically run for a long period of time, or for something that you want to run at a specific time every evening.

❷ PROTECT VARIANT: Checking this box will prevent anyone other than you from changing your variant. This can help prevent any surprises when you use your particular variant.

❸ HIDE FIELD: Checking certain fields in this column can help simplify your selection screen. Any field that you choose to hide will not appear on the selection screen in that variant, which can make the screen appear much simpler and more streamlined.

❹ SELECTION VARIABLE: My favorite use for selection variables is for dynamic dates. You can choose variables that will automatically choose dates for the report, depending on when you are running it. Additional variables can be defined as needed. Instead of saving a variant with the date 12/31/2015, you can use a variable that will set the date on the last day of the prior period.

4.1.2 Using a selection variant

Once you have created a selection variant, you or other users can utilize that variant to streamline your processes. To do that, you can click on the GET VARIANT button 🖺 or go to the menu path GOTO • VARIANTS • GET (⎇ + F5), as shown in Figure 4.4.

Figure 4.4: Menu path to get a variant

Choose your variant by double clicking on the desired line, or select it and click the CHOOSE button ☑ as shown in Figure 4.5. Then you can make any modifications needed for your selections and execute your report or transaction.

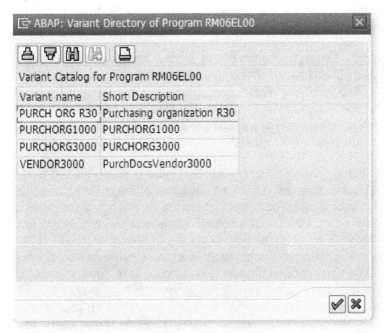

Figure 4.5: Choose a selection variant

4.2 Layouts

Next, I'll talk about how to create and use *layouts* for reports and line item displays. Layouts are great for customizing reports with specific fields, subtotaling, or sorting. This can help multiple users use the same transaction or report, but customize the resulting display to their individual needs.

4.2.1 Creating a layout

Now look at how to create a report layout using transaction FAGLB03 (G/L Account Line Item Display). This transaction is frequently used by many different members of an accounting department to review general ledger activity, but each of those users may want to view different pieces of data. They can use layouts to do that. SAP delivers several layouts, but also provides the ability to create your own.

To create a layout, once you've run a report, you can click on the CHANGE LAYOUT button ⊞, or use the menu path SETTINGS • LAYOUT • CURRENT. This will bring up a CHANGE LAYOUT window, as shown in Figure 4.6.

You'll see tabs ❶ across the top of this window for different components of the layout. The COLUMN SELECTION tab allows you to choose which columns to display in your report. SORT ORDER provides options to sort or subtotal on specific columns. FILTER lets you filter specific items in a column, either including them or excluding them. VIEW and DISPLAY lets you view the report in different formats.

Staying in the COLUMN SELECTION tab (in Figure 4.6), on the left is the DISPLAY COLUMNS area ❷. This area shows all of the columns currently displayed in your layout. The buttons at the top let you adjust the order of those columns. You can select a column name and move it up or down by one column ▲▼ or all the way to the top or bottom of the list ⬆⬇. You'll see the summation symbol ∑ at the top of the AGGREGATION column ❸. When you choose a quantity or amount field, you can click the box here to total that column in your report. Next, is the COLUMN SET ❹. This is the list of columns available for your report. Click on your chosen field name, then click the left arrow button ◄ ❺ to move it into your DISPLAYED COLUMNS area. Conversely, if there's a field in DISPLAYED COLUMNS that you don't want to see, you can select it and click the right arrow button ▶ ❻ to remove it from your report. Once you've finished your selections, click the ADOPT (ENTER) button ✅ ⑥ to view your report, or click 🔲 Save As... to save it.

Selecting multiple fields

 If you want to move multiple fields into or out of your DISPLAYED COLUMNS list, you don't have to do that one field at a time. To choose multiple fields, you can press the Ctrl key while you click on the individual fields (as shown in Figure 4.7). If you want to choose a block of fields, click on the first field, then hold down the ⇧ key as you select the last field in your block (Figure 4.8).

Figure 4.6: Change layout window

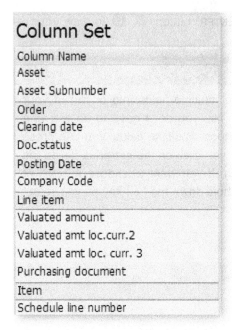

Figure 4.7: Selecting multiple entries in a list—Ctrl key

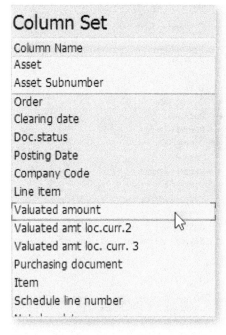

Figure 4.8: Selecting multiple entries in a list—Shift key

4.2.2 Modifying a layout

Once you've created your layout, you can display your report and modify your layout. You can go back to the CHANGE LAYOUT window from Figure 4.6, or you can make some modifications directly in the report screen. Some of these modifications will use the right-click context menu, and some will use the layout buttons from the application toolbar

In Figure 4.9, you can see the current report layout. You can see symbols in the column headings that show if the column is sorted in ascending order ❶ (red triangles pointing up), filtered ❷ (funnel), totaled ❸ (summation symbol), or sorted in descending order ❹ (red triangle pointing down).

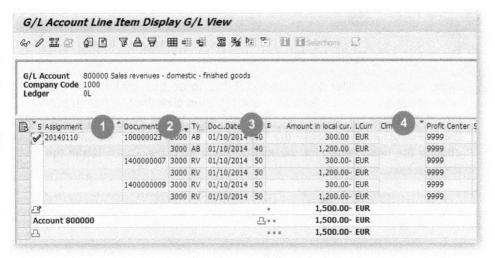

Figure 4.9: Current report layout with column heading symbols

Modifying a layout directly in the report screen

To demonstrate some of the options for modifying a layout directly in the report, you'll modify the layout shown in Figure 4.9. You will remove (hide) a column with no data, change a filter value, change the sort order on a column, and add subtotals.

First, remove the column for CLRNG DOC. To do this, you can click on the column heading, then right click for the context menu, and choose HIDE, as shown in Figure 4.10.

Figure 4.10: Hide column in a report layout

Next, remove the filter on DOCUMENT TYPE. To do this, click on the column heading to select it (see Figure 4.11), then click the SET FILTER button ⅋ (or press ⌈Ctrl⌉ + ⌈⇧⌉ + ⌈F2⌉). You want to see everything available in this column, so delete the filter that's already there. You can also change the filter values for multiple columns from the FILTER tab in the CHANGE LAYOUT screen.

Document...	BusA	Type	Doc..Date
1400000000	9900	RV	03/12/2015
1400000001	9900	RV	03/14/2015
1400000013	9900	RV	03/14/2015
1400000004	9900	RV	03/18/2015
1400000008	9900	RV	03/18/2015
1400000002	9900	RV	03/19/2015
1400000003	9900	RV	03/19/2015
1400000005	9900	RV	03/19/2015
1400000006	9900	RV	03/19/2015
1400000007	1000	RV	04/01/2015
1400000009	9900	RV	04/03/2015

Figure 4.11: Change filter in report layout

Now change the sort order in the report. One way to do this is to select a column heading, then click the appropriate sort button: ⏶ to sort ascending (0-9, A-Z) or ⏷ to sort descending (Z-A, 9-0). For more complex sorting scenarios, you can return to the CHANGE LAYOUT screen, and click on the SORT ORDER tab (see Figure 4.12). You can select and move columns similarly to the COLUMN SELECTION screen shown in Figure 4.6.

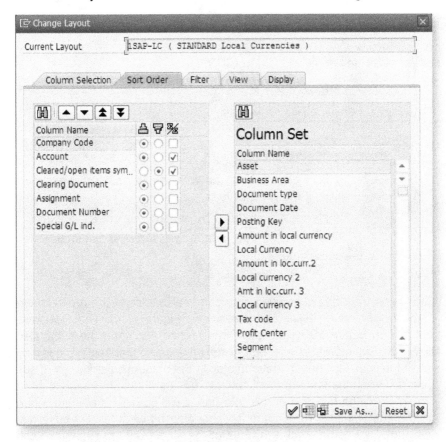

Figure 4.12: Change sort order in change layout window

In Figure 4.13, you can see a set of radio buttons and checkboxes to sort or subtotal on selected columns. This can let you sort or subtotal on more than one column at a time.

Figure 4.13: Sort and subtotal in change layout window

Subtotals in report layout

In your report, you can total the amount columns by clicking the DISPLAY SUM button ∑, and you can subtotal by specific columns by clicking the SUBTOTAL button ⅗. The SUBTOTAL button will sort and subtotal your column at the same time.

Once your report is subtotaled, you can use buttons in the report to expand or contract the subtotal levels (see Figure 4.14). The COLLAPSE SELECTION button ❶ will collapse that section and show the subtotaled line. The EXPAND SELECTION button ❷ will expand that section, showing all of the lines included in that subtotal. In the amount columns, you'll see dots showing the level of the subtotals ❸. As shown in Figure 4.14, if you click on the two dots on the total line, it will collapse the entire report to the subtotal lines (or expand it, depending on what levels you're displaying). You can also click on one of the single dots to expand or collapse that section.

04/06/2015	50		10.00- EUR
	50		20.00- EUR
04/06/20		▪	30.00- EUR
06/01		▪	300.00- EUR
12/14	50		26,000.00- EUR
12/14/2015		▪	26,000.00- EUR
12/31/2015	50		800,000.00- EUR
12/31/2015		▪	800,000.00- EUR
		▪ ▪	831,610.00- EUR

Figure 4.14: Subtotal levels

Once you've finished your changes, you will want to save your layout so that you or other users can use it in the future. You can do this in the CHANGE LAYOUT window, as discussed in the Creating a layout section. You can also click the SAVE LAYOUT button 🖫 to save it.

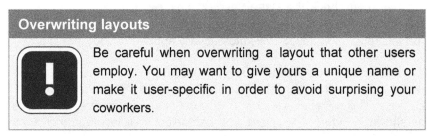

Overwriting layouts

Be careful when overwriting a layout that other users employ. You may want to give yours a unique name or make it user-specific in order to avoid surprising your coworkers.

4.2.3   Saving and retrieving a layout

Here are some tips to use when saving your new layout.

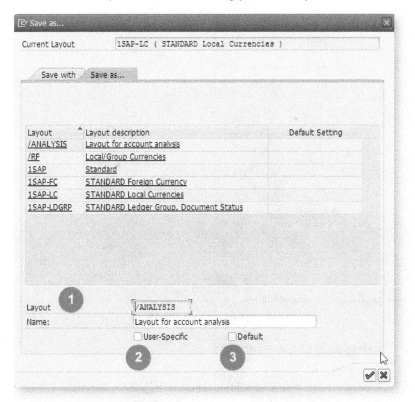

Figure 4.15: Save layout window

In the SAVE AS... window (Figure 4.15), the LAYOUT field ❶ is where you'll give your new layout a name. If you want to overwrite an existing layout, choose that layout. For a new layout, choose a new name for it. If you want your layout to be accessible only by you, and not by other users, you can check the USER-SPECIFIC box ❷. Checking the DEFAULT box ❸ will make this your default layout. That means that whenever you run this report, that layout will automatically appear for you.

To retrieve a layout, you can run your report, then click the SELECT LAYOUT button ⊞. You can also use the menu path SETTINGS • LAYOUT • CHOOSE. This will open a window with a list of all layouts available to you, as shown in Figure 4.16. Here, you can select your layout and click the ADOPT (ENTER) button ✅, or double click your chosen layout.

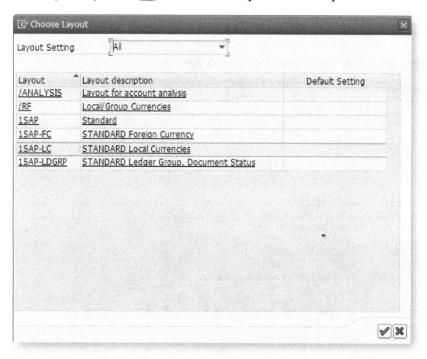

Figure 4.16: Choose layout window

4.3 Review and quick reference

This chapter covered more tips for personalizing SAP. Section 4.1 discussed how to create a selection variant, so you can run transactions or reports without re-entering the same selection criteria every time. Section

4.2 went over creating report layouts, which allow you to view a report in the same format every time, including sort order, filters, and totals. Figure 4.17 is a quick reference table with some of the buttons and keyboard shortcuts used in variants and layouts.

Button	Keyboard Shortcut	Function
	Shift + F5	Get variant: Choose a selection variant to automatically fill in selection fields. Use menu path to create and save a variant.
	Ctrl + F8	Change layout: Change the current report layout
	Ctrl + F9	Select layout: Choose an existing layout
	Ctrl + F12	Save layout: Save your existing layout
	Ctrl + Shift + F5	Sort in ascending order: Sorts the selected field or column
	Ctrl + Shift + F4	Sort in descending order: Sorts the selected field or column
	Ctrl + Shift + F2	Filter: Filter the selected field or column
	Shift + F7	Total: Totals the selected amount/quantity fields or columns
	Ctrl + F1	Subtotals: Sorts and subtotals the totaled fields by the selected fields or columns

Figure 4.17: Quick reference for buttons used in selection variants and report layouts

5 Exporting data

When working with a list or report, you may want to download or export it to make it available for offline analysis or distribution. Now that you've learned about using selection variants and layouts to run reports, you'll look at a few different methods to download or export a report. Some transactions may only offer a single method for exporting, but some will offer several. I'll review some of the options and how to find them, so that you can figure out which is the best option for your reporting needs. While it's possible to export to .html or word processing documents, I will focus on exporting to a spreadsheet.

5.1   Export

Exporting a file can provide a very quick and easy method for exporting a file directly to a spreadsheet or word processing document. Depending on the report or screen you're using, you might need to use a menu path or a button from the application toolbar. The options can be different depending on the module or report you're using. Explore the menus and buttons in your most-used transactions to see what is available and what method you prefer.

One common option is the menu path LIST • EXPORT • SPREADSHEET (see Figure 5.1). Another one you might see is the SPREADSHEET button ⬚. A third option is to right click in the report area, then select SPREADSHEET... in the context menu (see Figure 5.2).

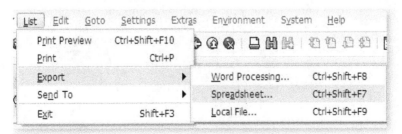

Figure 5.1: Menu path to export list as a spreadsheet

50	1,200.00- EUR		1,200.0
40	2,600.00 EUR		2,600.0
50	2,600.00- EUR		2.600.0
50	2,600.0(	Copy Text	500.0
50	2,600.0(	Optimize Width	500.0
40	2,809.0(	Find...	309.0
50	2,809.0(	Set Filter...	309.0
50	2,809.0(		309.0
50	26,000.0(	Spreadsheet...	300.0

Figure 5.2: Context (right click) menu for spreadsheet export

Next, you'll see the SELECT SPREADSHEET box, where you can choose the format for your exported spreadsheet (Figure 5.3). You can choose one of the formats shown ❶, or choose SELECT FROM ALL AVAILABLE FORMATS ❷, and use any of the formats shown in Figure 5.4. Once you know which format you prefer, you can check the ALWAYS USE SELECTED FORMAT box. That will default your selected format and let you skip this step for future exports.

Experiment with the different available formats and choose the one that works best for you. Most of them will automatically open in Excel (or your default spreadsheet program). I typically use the first option, EXCEL (IN MHTML FORMAT). It opens in Excel without changing your columns, sort order, and subtotals. Another useful option is EXCEL (IN EXISTING XXL FORMAT). It can allow you to export directly into a pivot table.

Changing your default format

What happens if you accidentally checked the ALWAYS USE SELECTED FORMAT box, or you want to change your mind? To reset your default spreadsheet format, you can right click in your report, then choose SPREADSHEET in the context menu (as shown in Figure 5.2).

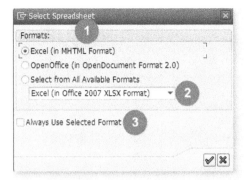

Figure 5.3: Select spreadsheet box

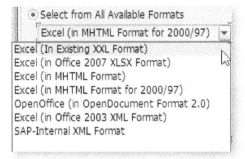

Figure 5.4: Available formats for exporting to spreadsheet

5.2 Save as local file

In some cases, when exporting directly to a spreadsheet isn't an option, you may need to save it as a local file. This option will let you save the file to your desktop or other location, but it will not automatically open up Excel as some of the export options do.

Saving as a local file is typically available through the menu path SYSTEM • LIST • SAVE • LOCAL FILE (see example in Figure 5.5). You'll then see the SAVE LIST IN FILE box (Figure 5.6), where you can choose the type of file to use. My choice is typically TEXT WITH TABS to save the report as a tab-delimited text file, then open it in Excel with minimal formatting and cleanup. Other good options are UNCONVERTED or IN THE CLIPBOARD; however, those require some cleanup in Excel, such as deleting empty rows or separating text into columns.

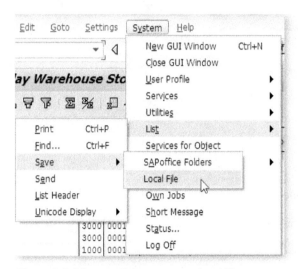

Figure 5.5: Menu path to save as a local file

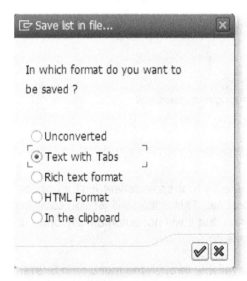

Figure 5.6: Save list in file box

5.3   Office integration

Another option available for some finance and controlling *Report Writer/Report Painter* reports is to use *Office Integration*. Office Integration effectively opens your report in Excel inside SAP (shown in Figure 5.8), rather than in its typical list format (shown in Figure 5.7). This can typically be used on transactions such as GR55 (EXECUTE REPORT GROUP) or reporting transactions starting with S_ALR_.

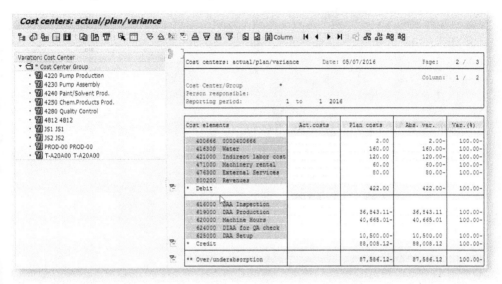

Figure 5.7: Sample cost center report without office integration

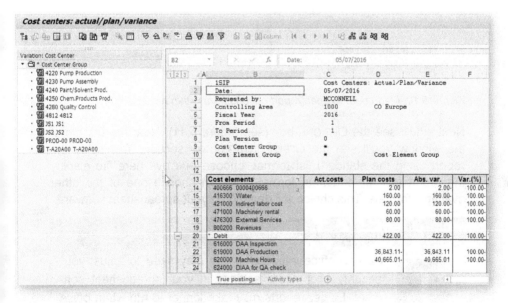

Figure 5.8: Sample cost center report with office integration

To use office integration, go to the menu path ENVIRONMENT • OPTIONS (see Figure 5.9) from the report selection screen. Alternately, from the report display, you can use the menu path SETTINGS • OPTIONS (see Figure 5.10).

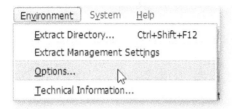

Figure 5.9: Menu path to open report options

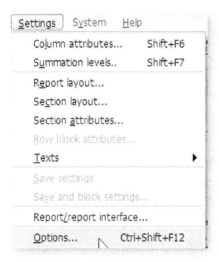

Figure 5.10: Menu path to open report options from within report display

Next, you'll see the OPTIONS box (see Figure 5.11). Near the bottom of the window you'll see the OFFICE INTEGRATION section. To display the report using the standard list format, choose INACTIVE here. To display the report in a spreadsheet format, you can choose one of the other available formats. This choice will depend on your spreadsheet software.

Spreadsheet software settings
To use office integration, you may need to adjust your security and macro settings in your spreadsheet software. Larger reports may take longer to run when office integration is turned on.

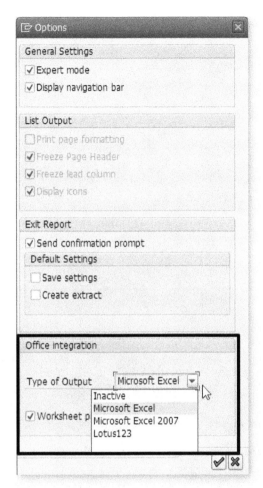

Figure 5.11: Report writer options for office integration

5.4 Review

Chapter 5 discussed different methods for exporting data from an SAP system to use in different formats, such as in a spreadsheet. You also reviewed the use of office integration, to see a report in Excel embedded in SAP.

6 Default values

As you work in an SAP system, you may find that you're entering the same information over and over again in different transactions. For example, you may have to enter the same company code or plant repeatedly. In this chapter, I'll discuss how you can set a default entry for some fields.

6.1 Parameter IDs

In the Menu bar section, you looked at the user profile, and how you could set your default printer, time zone, decimal notation, and date format. Also in the user record, there is a tab for PARAMETERS (as shown in Figure 6.1). This tab has three columns: ❶ SET/GET PARAMETER ID (the identification for the field for which you want to set a default value); ❷ PARAMETER VALUE (your default value for that field); and ❸ SHORT DESCRIPTION (the description of that parameter ID). Some parameters may be set by your system administrator. For those that aren't, you can find and set those parameters.

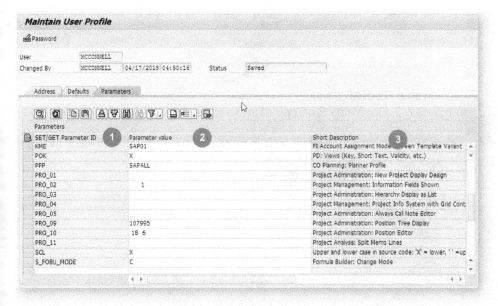

Figure 6.1: User profile parameters tab

Use the example of a sales representative who always enters sales orders for the same sales organization. Instead of entering the sales organization for every new sales order, you can default the sales organization by using parameters.

One way to find a parameter ID is to search using the same methodology as discussed in the Matchcode search tips section. However, this may not always give you a narrow enough result to easily choose the correct parameter ID. Start by searching for a parameter ID for sales organization. Figure 6.2 shows using wildcards to search for every parameter with 'sales org' in the description.

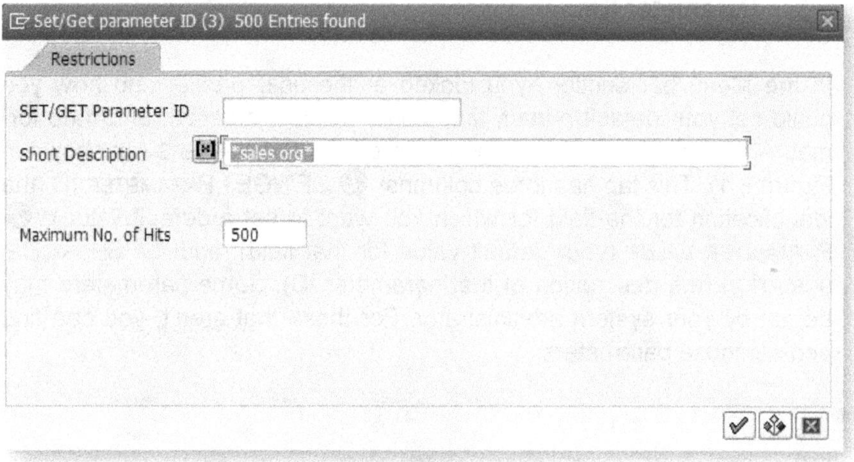

Figure 6.2: Parameter ID search for sales organization

This gives a list of all 'sales org' parameter IDs to choose from, as shown in Figure 6.3. Double click on one of these to select it.

Another way to find a parameter ID is to search directly from the field. In the example, you can start in transaction VA01 (Create Sales Order) as shown in Figure 6.4. Click on the SALES ORGANIZATION field, then click the HELP button ⑳ press F1 for the PERFORMANCE ASSISTANCE window. From that window, click the TECHNICAL INFORMATION button 👖.

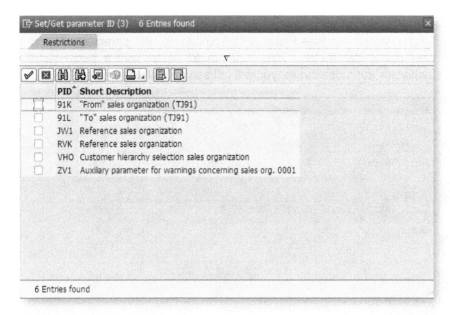

Figure 6.3: Available 'sales org' parameters

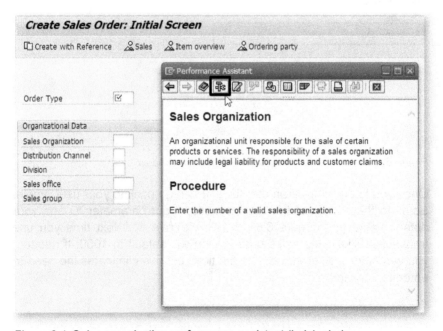

Figure 6.4: Sales organization performance assistant (help) window

In the TECHNICAL INFORMATION window, you'll see the PARAMETER ID in the FIELD DATA section (see Figure 6.5). You can use this parameter ID in the user profile parameters. Note that not all fields have a parameter ID available—for those cases, you will not see the parameter ID.

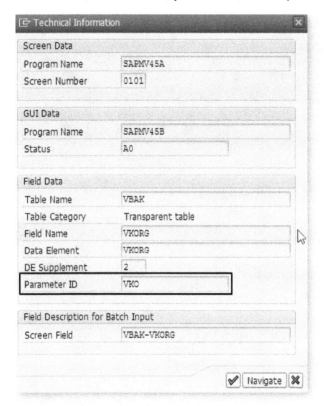

Figure 6.5: Parameter ID in technical information window

Once you know your parameter ID, you can go back to your user profile. Scroll to the bottom of the list, then enter your parameter ID and your default value (see Figure 6.6), then click save 🖫. Next time you use transaction VA01, the sales organization will default to 1000. If needed, you can enter a different value in the field, but this eliminates the need to enter it every time.

Figure 6.6: Parameter ID: New entry for sales organization

6.2 Other methods for setting default values

Some transactions will offer other methods for setting default values. Here are a few examples of where you can find these. As you work in an SAP system, look at the buttons and menu paths to see where else these options might be available.

6.2.1 Purchase order creation:

In transaction ME21N (Create Purchase Order), you'll see the DEFAULT VALUES button Default Values . Click this button to get the ITEM DEFAULT VALUES window, where you can select default values for purchase order creation (see Figure 6.7).

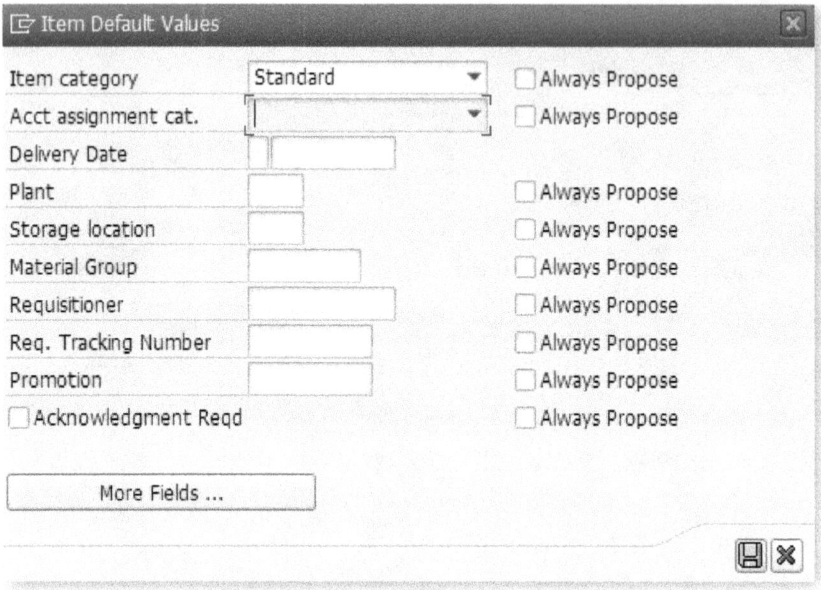

Figure 6.7: Purchase order item default values

6.2.2 Project builder

In transaction CJ20N (Project Builder), you can find default values for project builder functionality. To access these options, from CJ20N, follow the menu path SETTINGS • OPTIONS. You'll see the user-specific options window where you can define what you see in the project builder transaction, including how many projects appear in your history (see Figure 6.8).

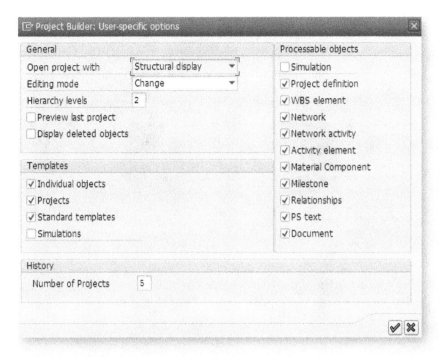

Figure 6.8: Project builder user options

6.2.3 Accounting editing options

Accounting editing options are available in several document editing transactions (such as entering G/L document, entering a customer invoice, or entering a vendor invoice). From these transactions, you can click the EDITING OPTIONS button ✐ Editing options or follow the menu path SETTING • PROCESSING OPTIONS. You can also access additional accounting editing options through transaction FB00 or from the SAP Easy Access menu path ACCOUNTING • FINANCIAL ACCOUNTING • GENERAL LEDGER • ENVIRONMENT • USER PARAMETERS • EDITING OPTIONS. As shown in Figure 6.9, this transaction provides a variety of default options for accounting functions, such as document entry, line item display, and document display.

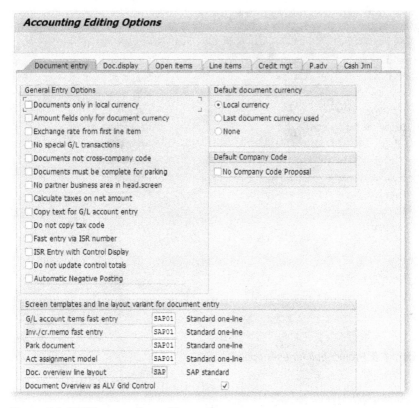

Figure 6.9: FB00 accounting editing options

6.2.4 Cost center accounting information system user settings

Similar to accounting editing options, cost center accounting information system user settings provides a central location where you can select defaults for all cost center accounting reports. To access it, you can use transaction RPC0, or the SAP Easy Access menu path ACCOUNTING • COST CENTER ACCOUNTING • INFORMATION SYSTEM • USER SETTINGS. As shown in Figure 6.10, you can set defaults for controlling area, cost center and groups, planning and reporting periods, and reporting currencies.

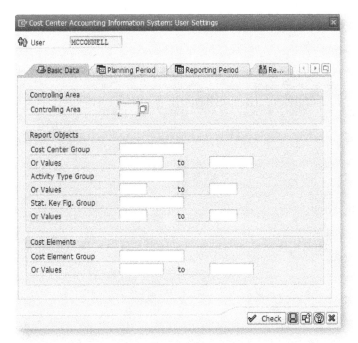

Figure 6.10: RPC0 cost center accounting information system user settings

6.3 Review

This chapter covered how to use parameter IDs to set default values for fields used frequently where you don't want to enter the same information every time, such as company code, plant, sales organization, etc. This chapter also showed how to get the parameter ID by using technical information ![icon] from the help window. Additionally, you looked at some specific functional transaction to set defaults for areas like purchase orders, projects, and financials.

7 Batch jobs, background jobs, and spool requests

In this chapter, I'll show some of SAP's options for processing or reporting large quantities of data, or how it can work when you're not logged in. First, I'll cover batch processing, when you might use it, and some introductory information on how to view and process jobs. Next, I'll share some basic tips for scheduling and monitoring background jobs. Finally, I'll review how to access and view your print spools.

7.1   Batch jobs

Batch jobs are typically used to enter data into an SAP system without requiring direct user interaction. One example could be when you need to load data from an external system, such as multiple ERP systems or an external payroll system. With the help of a developer, you can build an interface between your external system and your SAP system. That interface can automatically send data into your SAP system and perform actions like creating journal entries or updating master data. Another use of batch jobs could be transferring data from a legacy system to an SAP system during a new SAP implementation project.

Legacy system migration workbench

 Legacy system migration workbench (LSMW) is a tool provided by SAP to perform mass updates or migrations of data. It is typically used by IT analysts or developers, not by end users. LSMW provides some delivered update programs and it provides the functionality to record transactions and upload data files to make updates in SAP.

If you have responsibility to monitor or process batch jobs, I review some basic tips for doing so. Typically, an end user may not be directly creating the jobs, but they may monitor the jobs for errors.

The transaction code to monitor or process batch jobs is SM35, or you can use the SAP menu path TOOLS • ADMINISTRATION • MONITOR • BATCH INPUT. Depending on your authorizations, you'll see an overview of the batch jobs in your system (see Figure 7.1). You can narrow down your selection to specific jobs or users in the SELECTION CRITERIA section ❶. The SESSION NAME column ❷ will show you the name of the batch session or job. The ❸ status column has indicators showing whether the job is new and waiting to be processed ▢, if it was processed with errors ▨, or if it was processed successfully ☑. For jobs that have been processed (successfully or with errors), you can double click the job, or click the ❹ ANALYSIS ▣ Analysis or ❻ LOG ▤ Log buttons to view more information on the job, including document numbers created or errors that need to be corrected. For new jobs, you can select the job and click the ❺ PROCESS ⊕ Process button.

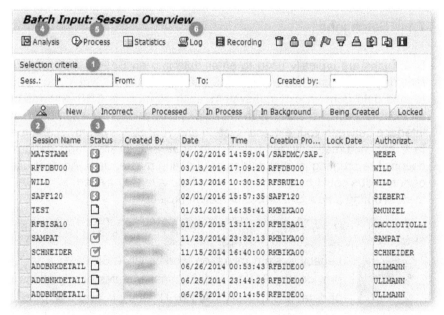

Figure 7.1: SM35 batch job overview screen

When you process a batch job in SM35, you will see a window with a choice of processing mode (see Figure 7.2). The first choice, PRO-CESS/FOREGROUND, will process your batch job immediately, and display each screen as it processes. The second choice, DISPLAY ERRORS ONLY, will process the job immediately, but will only display a screen if there is an error. This gives you the chance to correct any errors while the job is processing. The final option, BACKGROUND, processes the job in the background (sort of "behind the scenes"). Errors or success messages will show in the job log as the job completes.

Figure 7.2: Processing mode choices for batch processing

7.2 Background jobs

Background processing allows you to schedule jobs and reports to run at a specific time, perhaps overnight, when you are not logged into the system. Some examples of where you might want to use background processing include:

- ▶ Long running reports that time out
- ▶ Nightly jobs for MRP or invoicing
- ▶ Monthly settlement jobs that run sequentially
- ▶ Nightly sales or shipping reports
- ▶ Many others

7.2.1 Scheduling

To schedule a background job, you can usually use the menu path from the transaction you want to run. For example, look at how to schedule an inventory report (transaction MB52) to run in the background. Once you have entered your selection criteria, instead of clicking the execute ⊕ button to immediately execute the report, use the menu path PROGRAM • EXECUTE IN BACKGROUND (or keyboard shortcut F9), as shown in Figure 7.3.

Authorization to schedule background jobs

Check with your system administrator to verify that you have authorization to schedule and release background jobs. If you have authorization, the release will happen automatically, but this may need to be done by your administrator.

Menu path to execute in background

The first menu title won't always be PROGRAM. It will depend on the transaction you are running, and will be the first menu in the upper left corner of your screen.

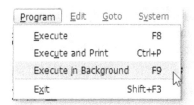

Figure 7.3: Menu path to run a job in the background

Next, you will typically see the BACKGROUND PRINT PARAMETERS window (see Figure 7.4). Here you can choose an output device (or printer), print format, and whether you want to print immediately or save it to the spool. Clicking on the PROPERTIES button `Properties` (`F9`) will show you additional property options. Double clicking on one of those options will let you change it, and give you the option to always show that property on your initial print parameter screen.

Print immediately or send to spooler?

If you're not sure how many pages your report will be, it's a good idea to choose SAP SPOOL ONLY FOR NOW in your PRINT TIME property. This will make it available for you to print or export later, but prevent you from accidentally printing hundreds of pages to a shared printer.

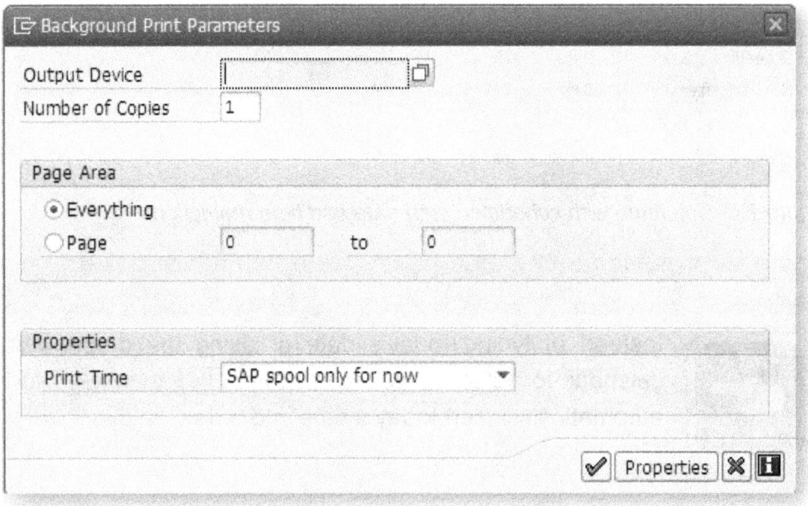

Figure 7.4: Background print parameters window

After you've set your print parameters and clicked the CONTINUE button ✔ (⬆ + F1), you'll see the START TIME window (Figure 7.11). This window provides numerous options for scheduling your job's start time, and will change depending on which button you choose. I'll review each of these options below, along with information on scheduling recurring jobs or setting restrictions.

Clicking the IMMEDIATE button [Immediate] will schedule your job to start immediately after you click SAVE 💾. The date/time section will display a checked box for IMMEDIATE START (see Figure 7.5).

Figure 7.5: Date/time section of start time window with immediate start selected

The DATE/TIME button [Date/Time] gives you the option of choosing a specific date and time for your job to start, and the option of restricting it to a certain time period. In Figure 7.6, you can see the job is scheduled to run on December 31, 2016 at 23:00:00 (11:00 PM). In the case of start delays, it is restricted so that it will not start after January 1, 2017 at midnight.

Date/Time				
Scheduled start	Date	12/31/2016	Time	23:00:00
No Start After	Date	1/1/2017	Time	00:00:00

Figure 7.6: Date/time with scheduled start date and time restrictions

Keyboard shortcut for choosing today's date

 Instead of typing today's date or using the dropdown calendar to select it, you can press F4 then F2 to automatically insert today's date into a date field.

Changing from a 24-hour clock to a 12-hour clock

 If you use the dropdown menu from the TIME field, you can click the SWITCH CLOCK button ⊙ to change from a 24-hour clock to a 12-hour clock, or vice versa.

The AFTER JOB button ⌐After job⌐ is useful when you need to run multiple jobs in succession. An example of this is an order settlement process, where you might need to run several jobs, each one dependent on the prior job. To use this, enter your first job name in the NAME field (see Figure 7.7). If you check the START STATUS-DEPENDENT BOX, that will ensure that the first job finishes before your next job starts. If the first job is cancelled for any reason, the second job will not start.

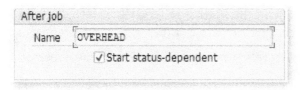

Figure 7.7: Schedule a job to run after a prior job has finished

> ### Scheduling multiple dependent jobs
>
> When you schedule your first job, schedule it with the DATE/TIME button [Date/Time] to start at a specific date and time in the future. Then you can schedule your subsequent jobs using the AFTER JOB button [After Job]. If the first job is already running, you won't have the option to schedule a job following it.

An *event* is a signal of some sort that a certain status or action has been completed. This can be a system event or user-defined event. For example, an event can be triggered when an external system has sent data to an SAP system to be processed. Clicking the AFTER EVENT button [After event] gives you the option to start your job after one of the events is triggered (see Figure 7.8).

After event	
Event	
Parameter	

Figure 7.8: Schedule a job to run after an event is triggered

Operation modes are set up by your system administrator to help manage your system resources. Examples could include normal operation or night operation. Clicking the AT OPERATION MODE button [At operation mode] will let you schedule your job to start when one of the operation modes is activated, as shown in Figure 7.9.

At operation mode	
Name	Night Operation

Figure 7.9: Schedule a job to run at a certain operation mode

In the next scheduling option, you can click the CONTINUE button ☐ to schedule jobs to run based on a *factory calendar* and workday. In Figure 7.10, the job is scheduled using FACTORY CALENDAR U.S. The WORKDAY is 1, and in this case is relative to the end of the month. This indicates that the job will run on the last day of the month. WORKDAY RELATIVE TO gives you the option to adjust and run jobs on a specific workday after the beginning of the month, or prior to the end of the month. The PERIOD section lets you schedule the job to recur every month. One example of where this is useful is in scheduling period closing jobs.

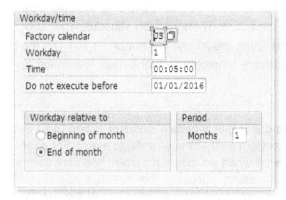

Figure 7.10: Schedule a job to run on the last workday of the month

Factory calendar

A factory calendar is usually created by your system administrators and defines the working and non-working days for your business, including days of the week and holidays.

At the bottom of the START TIME window is a check box for PERIODIC JOB (see Figure 7.11). If you check this box for a job scheduled immediately or at a certain date and time, you will also see buttons for PERIOD VALUES (F5) and RESTRICTIONS (F6) | Period Values || Restrictions |.

The PERIOD VALUES window (Figure 7.12) gives you the choice to repeat the job hourly, daily, weekly, monthly, or to choose other periods. The OTHER PERIOD button | Other period | gives you the flexibility to enter a quantity for any of those values. For example, you can choose to repeat the job every 2 weeks, as shown in Figure 7.13.

RESTRICTIONS will let you change the scheduling behavior based on a factory calendar. For example, if you want your job to run every Monday, but not on holidays, you can specify the holiday restriction in this window (Figure 7.14).

112

Figure 7.11: Start time scheduling window with periodic job flag

Figure 7.12: Period values for scheduling background jobs

Figure 7.13: Use other periods to schedule every 2 weeks

Figure 7.14: Start date restrictions: Do not run the job on Sundays or holidays in the U.S. factory calendar

---

Define background jobs in transaction SM36

 Another option is available to schedule background jobs, but this is typically used by system administrators rather than end users. In transaction SM36 (or through menu path SYSTEM • SERVICES • JOBS • DEFINE JOB), you can define jobs, including multiple steps or programs, without entering the original transaction code. It also offers a job wizard to help schedule jobs.

7.2.2 Monitoring

A couple of transactions to monitor your background jobs include SMXX and SM37. SMXX will go directly to the JOB OVERVIEW screen and display your jobs. It can also be accessed through the menu path SYSTEM • OWN JOBS, as shown in Figure 7.15. SM37 will allow you to choose which background jobs to display (depending on your level of authorization). SM37 is also accessible through the menu path SYSTEM • SERVICES • JOBS • JOB OVERVIEW.

Figure 7.15: Menu path to display your own jobs

The selection screen for SM37 provides multiple options to find a background job, as shown in Figure 7.16. First, if you know the job name you want to review, you can enter it in the JOB NAME ❶ field. If you don't know it, you can use an asterisk * as a wild card. You can also enter a specific USER NAME ❷ or wild card. This field will typically default with your own username, but you can overwrite this if you need to review other users' jobs. In the JOB STATUS section ❸, you can specify which status you want to review. For example, you may want to review jobs that have been completed, in which case you would check the FINISHED checkbox and leave the others blank. The JOB START CONDITION section ❹ lets you specify certain dates or times to review, or to review jobs that happened after a certain event. In some cases, you may want to review jobs that ran for a certain transaction or program. For those, you can enter the ABAP PROGRAM NAME in the JOB STEP section ❺. If you require additional selection criteria, you can click the EXTENDED JOB SELECTION ⋈Extended Job Selection button ❻ to get additional choices.

Finding the ABAP program name

In most cases, you can find the ABAP program name for a transaction in your status bar (Figure 7.17) or through menu path SYSTEM • STATUS in the REPOSITORY DATA section of the status window (Figure 7.18).

Simple Job Selection

⊕Execute   ⋈Extended Job Selection ❻   ℹ Information

Job name   ❶ | * |
User name   ❷ | * |

Job status ❸
☑Sched.   ☑Released   ☑Ready   ☑Active   ☑Finished   ☑Canceled

Job start condition ❹
From 🗓 06/01/2016   To 🗓 06/30/2016
From 🕐 [   ]   To 🕐 [   ]

or after event: [▾]

Job step ❺
ABAP program name: [   ]

Figure 7.16: Selection screen for transaction SM37

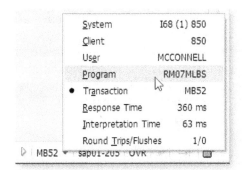

Figure 7.17: Status bar dropdown menu to view ABAP program name

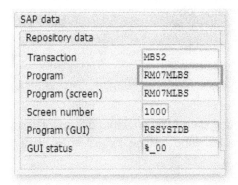

Figure 7.18: Repository data section of system status menu showing the ABAP program name

After you've completed your selection criteria and executed the transaction, you will see a list with data on all of the jobs you selected (see Figure 7.19). This list is displayed immediately if you've used transaction SMXX.

Job Overview

Job	Spool	Job Doc	Job CreatedB	Status	Start date	Start time	Duration(sec.)	
MMPV OPEN CURRENT PERIOD				Scheduled			0	
RM07MLBS	🖨			Finished	06/15/2016	17:21:00	121	
*Summary							121	

Figure 7.19: Job overview list

As with many report transactions in SAP, you can change the layout and sort the list by different columns. You can also select a job by checking the box next to it and review the spool (to be discussed in the Spool section), the job log, and the steps comprising that job. If you have an active job that you are waiting to complete, you can click the REFRESH button  to refresh the status as it runs. To compare the run time of a daily or weekly job, you can review the start and end times and duration of each job. If you have an active job that you want to stop running before completion, click the STOP ACTIVE JOBS button 🛑 to cancel it.

7.3   Spool requests

A SPOOL REQUEST is any document that has had a print function selected. These can be generated by background jobs where you've specified print parameters, clicking the PRINT button 🖨 in a transaction, or other processes that generate some sort of print job.

Printer options

❗ If you've chosen the printer output option to delete immediately after printing (see Figure 7.20), your spool will be immediately deleted, and will no longer show in a spool list.

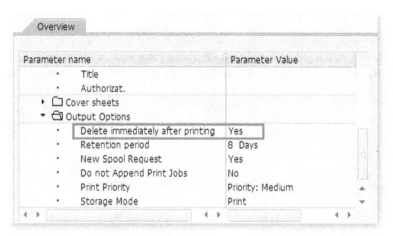

Figure 7.20: Printer output options: delete immediately after printing

For background jobs, you can access your spool request directly from SM37 or SMXX. If your job has a spool request, it will have a button that looks like a scroll of paper in the SPOOL column. To display the spool, first select the job, then click the SPOOL button 📜Spool (Figure 7.21).

Job	Spool	Job Doc	Job CreatedB	Status	Start date	Start time	Duration(sec.)	
MMPV OPEN CURRENT PERIOD				Scheduled			0	
RM07MLBS	📜			Finished	06/15/2016	17:21:00	121	
*Summary							121	

Job Overview

Figure 7.21: Spool indicator in job overview list

If your spool request was created by a process other than a background job, you can access your own spool lists through transaction SP02 or menu path SYSTEM • OWN SPOOL REQUESTS (see Figure 7.25). This will take you directly to a list of all of your spool requests.

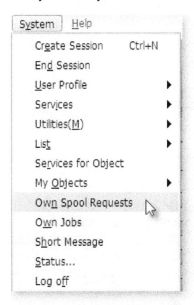

Figure 7.22: Menu path to view your own spool requests

To view other users' spool requests, use transaction SP01 or menu path SYSTEM • SERVICES • OUTPUT CONTROL. This will take you to a selection screen (shown in Figure 7.23) where you can enter criteria to choose which spools to review. This selection screen gives you similar choices as many other SAP reports, such as the MULTIPLE SELECTION ⇨ and SELECTION OPTIONS 🦋 buttons.

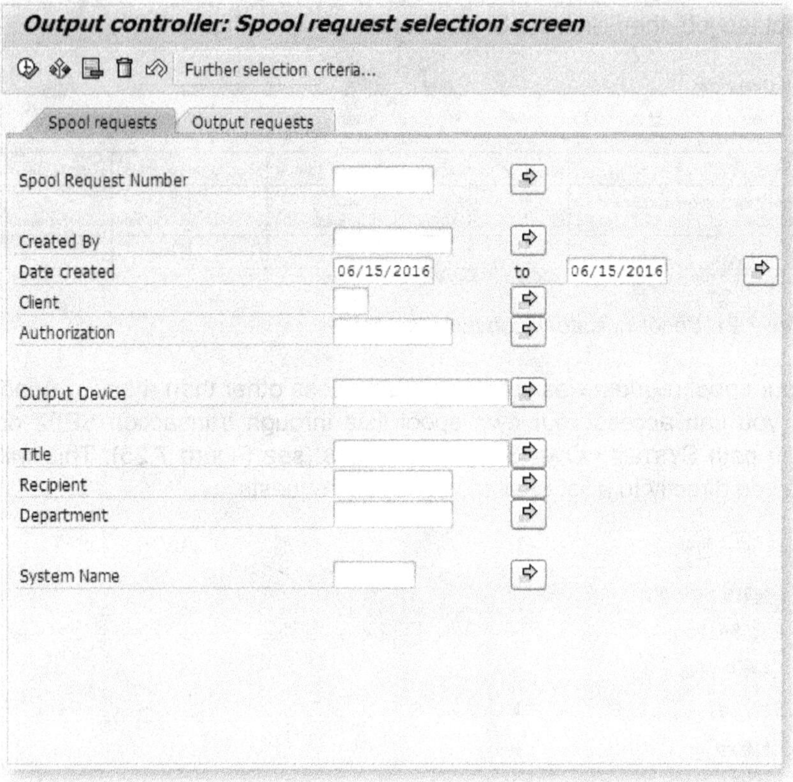

Figure 7.23: Output controller selection screen

Next (after using SP01, SP02, SMXX, or SM37 to find the spool requests), you'll see the OUTPUT CONTROLLER: LIST OF SPOOL REQUESTS screen, shown in Figure 7.24. To view a spool, you can either select the list and click the ABAP LIST button 📖, click the DISPLAY CONTENTS button 👓, press ⌐F6⌐, or use the menu path GOTO • DISPLAY REQUESTS • CONTENTS (shown in Figure 7.25). From that display, you can export the report, review it, or print it.

Output Controller: List of Spool Requests

Spool no.	Type	User	Date	Time	Status	Pages	Title	ODev	Immediate
6221				16:22	-	806	LIST1S LOCL RM07MLBS_SMC	LOCL	
427				15:53	Waiting	1	LIST1S LP01 RSBDCTL6_SMC	LP01	X
426				15:50	Waiting	1	LIST1S LP01 RSBDCTL6_SMC	LP01	X
425				15:46	Waiting	1	LIST1S LP01 RSBDCTL6_SMC	LP01	X
424				15:38	Waiting	1	LIST1S LP01 RSBDCTL6_SMC	LP01	X
423				15:24	Waiting	1	LIST1S LP01 RSBDCTL6_SMC	LP01	X
422				15:10	Waiting	1	LIST1S LP01 RSBDCSUB_SMC	LP01	X
421				14:56	Waiting	1	LIST1S LP01 RSBDCSUB_SMC	LP01	X
420				14:56	Waiting	1	LIST1S LP01 RSBDCTL6_SMC	LP01	X
419				14:48	Waiting	1	LIST1S LP01 RSBDCSUB_SMC	LP01	X
418				14:48	Waiting	1	LIST1S LP01 RSBDCTL6_SMC	LP01	X
417				14:47	Waiting	1	LIST1S LP01 RSBDCSUB_SMC	LP01	X
416				14:47	Waiting	1	LIST1S LP01 RSBDCTL6_SMC	LP01	X
20675				00:00	Waiting	3	LIST1S LP01 RMMMPERI_SMC	LP01	X
20219				00:00	Waiting	3	LIST1S LP01 RMMMPERI_SMC	LP01	X
19852				00:00	Waiting	3	LIST1S LP01 RMMMPERI_SMC	LP01	X
19307				00:00	Waiting	3	LIST1S LP01 RMMMPERI_SMC	LP01	X
18650				00:00	Waiting	3	LIST1S LP01 RMMMPERI_SMC	LP01	X
17985				00:00	Waiting	3	LIST1S LP01 RMMMPERI_SMC	LP01	X

```
19 Spool requests displayed

 1 Spool request w/o output request
18 Spool requests being processed
```

Figure 7.24: Output controller list of spool requests

Goto	Utilities(M)	Settings	System	Help		
Display requests	▶	Contents		F6		
Request attributes	F8	Settings...	Ctrl+Shift+F10			
Overview		Display current position				
Output requests	F5	Display graphically				
Where-Used List	Shift+F12	Display raw				
Next Request		Display hexadecimally				
Previous request						
Selection screen						
Back	F3					

Figure 7.25: Menu path to display spool request contents

Number of pages displayed in spool

 When you display a spool, you may see a message similar to the one in Figure 7.26, indicating that not all of the spool pages are displayed. You can change this by going to the menu path GOTO • DISPLAY REQUESTS • SETTINGS, pressing `Ctrl` + `⇧` + `F10`, or clicking the SETTINGS button `Settings...` . As shown in Figure 7.27, you can change the number of pages that are displayed in the DISPLAY AREA section. The SAVE SETTINGS section will let you change that setting for this transaction, for the session you're in, or permanently change the setting. Be cautious with that, as it can affect system performance.

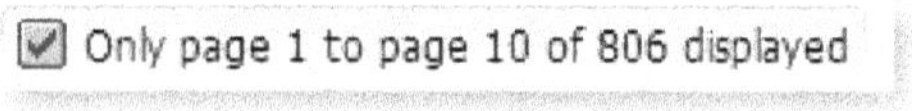

☑ Only page 1 to page 10 of 806 displayed

Figure 7.26: Message about limited pages displayed in spool

Display Mode
- ⦿ Graphical
- ○ Raw
- ○ Hexadecimal

Display area
- ⦿ From page | 1 | To page | 10
- ○ The last | 10 | pages

Save settings
- ⦿ Temp. for transaction
- ○ Temp. for session
- ○ Permanently even betw. logons

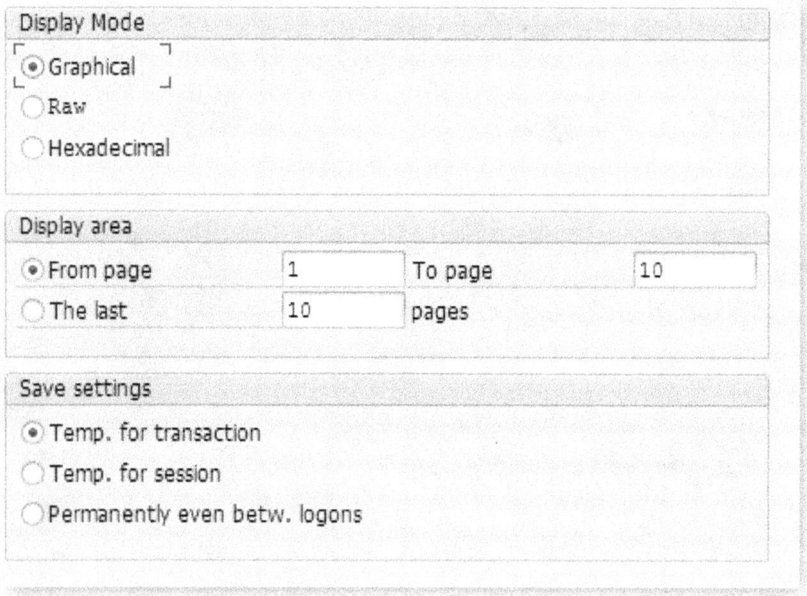

Figure 7.27: Spool display settings

If you know you would like to send or export the spool, you can do that without displaying the spool first. Select the spool by checking the box, then use the menu path SPOOL REQUEST • FORWARD, then choosing one of the available options in that menu.

7.4 Review

In this chapter, you looked at ways to use SAP to process information in batch processing or in the background, and when you might use either of those options. You also reviewed how to access a spool request for any list or report for which you've established print options.

8 Working with tables

Working with tables in SAP is something typically reserved for IT analysts or developers. However, there are cases (depending on your company's policies and procedures) where it can be helpful to have some simple tips for using tables. I'll discuss a few of those here. Note that SAP has hundreds of tables for master data, document headers, line items, configuration, etc. I am going to cover a few very basic tips on looking at master data tables. For many users, viewing or querying table data can help keep track of master data and make sure that data is being updated and managed correctly.

8.1 Table and field names

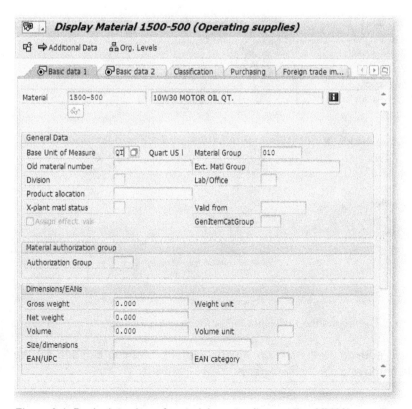

Figure 8.1: Basic data view of material master (transaction MM03)

In Section 6.1, you looked at the technical information for a field to determine the parameter ID. You can also use the technical information
window to determine table and field names for a particular field. As an
example, look at the basic data view in the material master (transaction
MM03), shown in Figure 8.1.

If you want to find out the table and technical field name for BASE UNIT OF
MEASURE, you can click on that field, press F1 to get the PERFORMANCE
ASSISTANT (help) window (see Figure 8.2), then click the TECHNICAL IN-
FORMATION button .

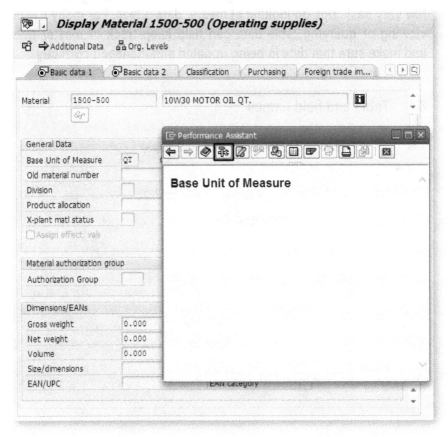

Figure 8.2: Performance assistant window for base unit of measure

In the TECHNICAL INFORMATION window (Figure 8.3), you can see ❶ the
table name and ❷ the field name.

Figure 8.3: Technical information for base unit of measure

In some cases, the data you want may be in a table, but you can't find the table name through this method. Here is a short list (Figure 8.4) of a few useful tables and descriptions that are more challenging to find:

Table name	Description	Function
TSTC	SAP transaction codes	List of all transaction codes and their description
STXH	SAPscript text file header	List of objects with long text
DD02T	SAP data dictionary table texts	List of SAP tables and descriptions
UST04	User masters	List of users and profiles
VARI	ABAP/4: Variant storage	List of selection variants
CVERS	Release status of software components in system	List of all system components and their current version
CDHDR	Change document header	With CDPOS, displays all change documents in system
CDPOS	Change document items	With CDHDR, displays all change documents in system

Figure 8.4: Short list of useful tables

127

8.2   Viewing table contents

Once you know the table name, you can view or query the table to find other information. There are a couple of ways to do this, depending on your system settings and authorizations.

The first is to go to GENERAL TABLE DISPLAY (transaction SE16N). Here, you can enter the table name you found in the technical information (see Figure 8.5). Some of the other criteria and settings available in general table display (Figure 8.5) include:

1. SELECTION CRITERIA: Here you can enter additional selection criteria to narrow down your selection, using the tips discussed in Section 2.2.2.

2. MAXIMUM NO. OF HITS: This is the maximum number of items that will be displayed in your list. You can update this as needed (keeping in mind that a longer list can result in a longer runtime).

3. EXECUTE ⊕: Click this to start your list.

4. BACKGROUND: Click this button to run your list in the background.

5. NUMBER OF ENTRIES: After you enter all of your selection criteria, you can click this button to find out how many entries exist for that selection, then decide if you need to increase the maximum number of hits.

6. TECHNICAL SETTINGS: This button opens the technical settings window, where you can change your default display settings (see Figure 8.6).

7. WHERE-USED LIST: This button can show you all of the programs, screens, and other technical objects that use the table selected.

Background processing

 Some reports and transactions provide the option of executing or scheduling them to run using background processing. This is particularly useful for long-running transactions, or transactions you want to run during non-work hours. You can view these jobs and download the results with transaction SM37 (Job Overview).

Figure 8.5: General table display (SE16N)

Figure 8.6: General table display technical settings

SAP Query and Quickviewer

 SAP Query (transaction SQ01) and Quickviewer (SQVI) are query tools that can be used to join and view tables without custom coding. Depending on your company's security settings, these can be relatively quick and easy tools to use for reporting on data in tables.

8.3 Review

In this chapter, you took a very basic look at some highly technical information: how to find and view tables. You also found another use for the TECHNICAL INFORMATION button 🔳 to determine table and field names.

9 Authorizations

Authorizations and security are generally managed by your system administrator or security group. In this chapter, I'll show you some basic tips on how to report authorization errors and how to view transactions and roles assigned to users.

9.1 Authorization errors

At times you may receive an authorization error when trying to access or run a transaction. The error will typically read something like "You are not authorized to..." When you get this error, your system administrator may ask you to send additional information, typically from transaction SU53 (DISPLAY AUTHORIZATION DATA FOR USER). To run this, it is usually best to run transaction /NSU53 or /OSU53 immediately after getting the authorization error, then send a screen shot of the results to your system administrator (see Figure 9.1).

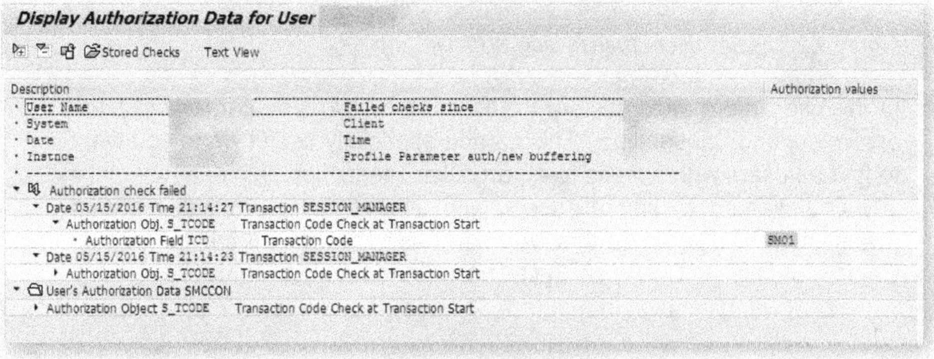

Figure 9.1: SU53 display authorization data for user

9.2 View user roles and transactions

To view the roles and transaction authorizations assigned to a user, you can use transaction SU01D (DISPLAY USERS) or transaction SUIM (USER INFORMATION SYSTEM).

In transaction SU01D, you can click on the ROLES tab to see a list of the security roles assigned to that user (see Figure 9.2). You can drill into those roles to get additional details such as the transactions provided through those roles.

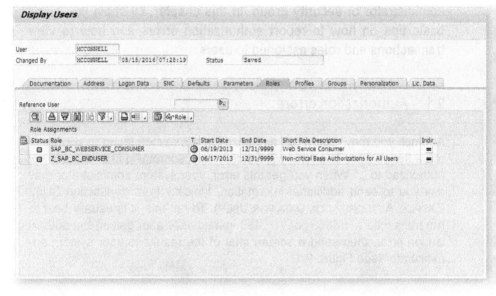

Figure 9.2: Display users (transaction SU01D)

In the user information system (transaction SUIM), you can analyze users, roles, and transactions. This can be especially useful when you want to find all users with access to a particular transaction. For example, let's say you wanted to find all users with access to create sales orders (transaction VA01). To do this, you can navigate through the menu path USER • USERS BY COMPLEX SELECTION CRITERIA • BY TRANSACTION AUTHORIZATIONS, as shown in Figure 9.3.

Enter transaction VA01 in the TRANSACTION CODE field, then click the EXECUTE button ⊕ (see Figure 9.4) to see a list of all users who can create a sales order with transaction VA01.

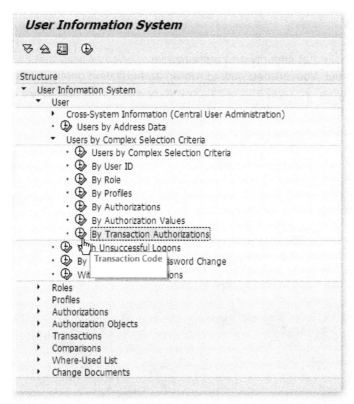

Figure 9.3: User information system: Users by transaction authorizations

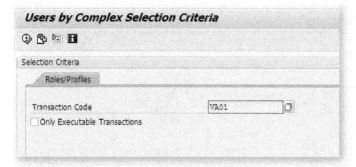

Figure 9.4: Users by complex selection criteria

9.3 Review

This chapter looked at security and authorizations, another area that can be quite technical. You learned how to run an authorization check (transaction SU53) when you get authorization errors, along with how to do a basic analysis of security roles and assignments.

10 Quick reference

This final chapter will have quick references to information covered throughout the book.

10.1 System function bar buttons

Button	Keyboard shortcut (Hotkey)	Function
	Enter	Enter, confirm data
	Ctrl + S	Save
	F3	Back
	Shift + F3	Exit
	F12	Cancel
	Ctrl + P	Print
	Ctrl + F	Find
	Ctrl + G	Find next
	Ctrl + PgUp	First page
	PgUp	Previous page
	PgDn	Next page
	Ctrl + PgDn	Last page
	None	Creates new session
	None	Generates a shortcut
	F1	Help
	Alt + F12	Customize local layout

Figure 10.1: System function bar buttons and keyboard shortcuts

10.2 SAP menu buttons

Button/icon	Keyboard shortcut (Hotkey)	Function
	Ctrl + F10	User menu
	Ctrl + F11	SAP menu
	Ctrl + F12	SAP Business Workplace
	Ctrl + Shift + F6	Add to favorites
	Shift + F2	Delete favorites
	Ctrl + Shift + F3	Change favorites
		Favorite transaction
 ▸ ☐		Closed (collapsed) menu section
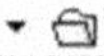 ▾ ☐		Open (expanded) menu section
 • ⬡		Transaction node

Figure 10.2: SAP menu buttons

10.3 Command field entries and shortcuts

Entry	Function
/N	Go to SAP menu without saving data
/Ntcode	Go to a new transaction without saving data
/O	Display session list, open new session
/Otcode	Go to a new transaction in a new session
/I	Close current session
/NEND	Log off and exit all with prompt to save data
/NEX	Log off and exit all without saving data
SU53	Authorization check info (with /N or /O)
SU3	User profile
SU02	View your spool requests
SMXX	View your background jobs
SM35	Batch job processing
	Command field – click down arrow for history

Figure 10.3: Command field entries and shortcuts

10.4 Selection and reporting buttons

Button(s)	Function
	Get selection variant
	Execute report or transaction
	Get details on line item
	Sort ascending or descending (select column first)
	Filter (select column first)
	Summation (total) for amount or quantity columns
	Subtotal: click on column for subtotal criteria
	Export to spreadsheet
	Export to word processing document
	Save to local file
	Manage report layouts

Figure 10.4: Selection and reporting buttons

You have finished the book.

A The Author

Sydnie McConnell is the lead SAP business systems analyst for a global manufacturing firm headquartered in Colorado. Sydnie has more than 15 years of experience with SAP Financials, both as a business user and a systems analyst. Her primary focus is on SAP Controlling, particularly product cost controlling and profitability analysis. She has worked on a variety of complex projects, including several global SAP ERP and BPC implementations and integrating multiple ERP systems into a single SAP general ledger.

B Index

C Disclaimer

This publication contains references to the products of SAP SE.

SAP, R/3, SAP NetWeaver, Duet, PartnerEdge, ByDesign, SAP BusinessObjects Explorer, StreamWork, and other SAP products and services mentioned herein as well as their respective logos are trademarks or registered trademarks of SAP SE in Germany and other countries.

Business Objects and the Business Objects logo, BusinessObjects, Crystal Reports, Crystal Decisions, Web Intelligence, Xcelsius, and other Business Objects products and services mentioned herein as well as their respective logos are trademarks or registered trademarks of Business Objects Software Ltd. Business Objects is an SAP company.

Sybase and Adaptive Server, iAnywhere, Sybase 365, SQL Anywhere, and other Sybase products and services mentioned herein as well as their respective logos are trademarks or registered trademarks of Sybase, Inc. Sybase is an SAP company.

SAP SE is neither the author nor the publisher of this publication and is not responsible for its content. SAP Group shall not be liable for errors or omissions with respect to the materials. The only warranties for SAP Group products and services are those that are set forth in the express warranty statements accompanying such products and services, if any. Nothing herein should be construed as constituting an additional warranty.

More Espresso Tutorials Books

Boris Rubarth:

First Steps in ABAP®

► Step-by-Step instructions for beginners

► Comprehensive descriptions and code examples

► A guide to create your first ABAP application

► Tutorials that provide answers to the most commonly asked programming questions

http://5015.espresso-tutorials.com

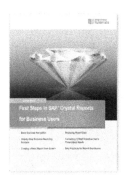

Anurag Barua:

First Steps in SAP® Crystal Reports for Business Users

► Basic end-user navigation

► Creating a basic report from scratch

► Formatting to meet individual presentation needs

http://5017.espresso-tutorials.com

Claudia Jost:

First Steps in the SAP® Purchasing Processes (MM)

► Compact manual for the SAP procurement processes

► Comprehensive example with numerous illustrations

► Master data, purchase requirements and goods receipt in context

http://5016.espresso-tutorials.com

Björn Weber:

First Steps in the SAP® Production Processes (PP)

- ▶ Compact manual for discrete production in SAP
- ▶ Comprehensive example with numerous illustrations
- ▶ Master data, resource planning and production orders in context

http://5027.espresso-tutorials.com

Sydnie McConnell & Martin Munzel:

First Steps in SAP® (2nd, extended edition)

- ▶ Learn how to navigate in SAP ERP
- ▶ Learn about transactions, organizational units, master data
- ▶ Watch instructional videos with simple, step-by-step examples
- ▶ Get an overview of SAP products and new development trends

http://5045.espresso-tutorials.com

Ashish Sampat:

First Steps in SAP® Controlling (CO)

- ▶ Cost center and product cost planning and actual cost flow
- ▶ Best practices for cost absorption using Product Cost Controlling
- ▶ Month-end closing activities in SAP Controlling
- ▶ Examples and screenshots based on a case study approach

http://5069.espresso-tutorials.com

Gerardo di Giuseppe:

First Steps in SAP® Business Warehouse (BW)

- ▶ Tips for Loading Data to SAP BW with SAP ETL
- ▶ Using Business Content to Accelerate your BW objects
- ▶ How to Automate ETL Tasks Using Process Chains
- ▶ Leverage BEx Query Designer and BEx Analyzer

http://5088.espresso-tutorials.com

Ann Cacciottolli:

First Steps in SAP® Financial Accounting (FI)

- ▶ Overview of key SAP Financials functionality and SAP ERP integration
- ▶ Step-by-step guide to entering transactions
- ▶ SAP Financials reporting capabilities
- ▶ Hands-on instruction based on examples and screenshots

http://5095.espresso-tutorials.com

www.ingramcontent.com/pod-product-compliance
Lightning Source LLC
Chambersburg PA
CBHW071207050326

40689CB00011B/2264